The Dover Opera Libretto Series

PUCCINI'S
MADAMA BUTTERFLY

GIACOMO PUCCINI, *1858-1924*

Translated and Edited by
STANLEY APPELBAUM

027218

DOVER PUBLICATIONS, INC.
NEW YORK

Copyright © 1983 by Dover Publications, Inc.
All rights reserved under Pan American and International Copyright Conventions.

Published in Canada by General Publishing Company, Ltd., 30 Lesmill Road, Don Mills, Toronto, Ontario.
Published in the United Kingdom by Constable and Company, Ltd., 10 Orange Street, London WC2H 7EG.

This Dover edition, first published in 1983, contains the Italian text of the first orchestral score (1907), together with a complete English translation prepared especially for Dover Publications by Stanley Appelbaum, who has also written the Introduction, List of Characters, Plot Summary and Translator's Notes.

Manufactured in the United States of America
Dover Publications, Inc., 180 Varick Street, New York, N.Y. 10014

Library of Congress Cataloging in Publication Data

Puccini, Giacomo, 1858–1924.
    [Madama Butterfly.   Libretto.   English & Italian]
    Puccini's Madama Butterfly.

    (The Dover opera libretto series)
    English and Italian.
    Based on: Madame Butterfly / David Belasco.
    Libretto by Luigi Illica and Giuseppe Giacosa.
    1. Operas—Librettos.   I. Appelbaum, Stanley.   II. Illica, Luigi, 1857–1919.   III. Giacosa, Giuseppe, 1847–1906.   IV. Belasco, David, 1853–1931.   Madame Butterfly.   V. Title.   VI. Title: Madama Butterfly.   VII. Series.
    ML50.P965M22   1983   782.1'2   82-18195
    ISBN 0-486-24465-2

CONTENTS

INTRODUCTION

In *Madama Butterfly*, Giacomo Puccini (1858–1924), inheritor of Verdi's mantle as master of the Italian lyric stage, created one of his three most popular and most frequently performed operas. The story has wide appeal. The heroine's role is the most fully developed, both psychologically and musically, in all of the composer's works. His lavish Italian melody is here intriguingly spiced with real or simulated Japanese tunes, and the orchestration is particularly delicate and refined. The genesis of this masterpiece is a fascinating tale in itself.

The short story "Madame Butterfly" by John Luther Long first appeared in the January 1898 issue of *The Century*. Long (1861–1927), a lawyer in Philadelphia, received background information for a number of stories (and, later, plays) set in Japan from his sister, the wife of a missionary resident there. For "Madame Butterfly" in particular, he was also clearly inspired by Pierre Loti's novel *Madame Chrysanthème* of 1887, which had already dealt with the temporary Japanese "wife" of an Occidental naval officer, although Chrysanthemum was worldly and opportunistic, rather than fragile, naïve and willfully blind to her real situation like Butterfly. Adaptations of Japanese motifs in all the Western arts were modish, in fact commonplace, by 1898, and Long's story was well received (except by naval officers, who bombarded him with irate letters), being reprinted in volume form several times.

The great master of stagecraft and realistic melodrama David Belasco (ca. 1853–1931) no doubt recognized that a dramatization of the story, with its combination of pathos and broad humor, would provide a capital role for Blanche Bates, the vivacious actress he was currently nurturing for stardom; she would have the opportunity to stride and "cuss" like a man in her parrot-like reminiscences of Pinkerton's ways, and she would speak in that atrocious jargon larded with malapropisms. Thus, the play *Madame Butterfly* became the first of several Belasco-Long collaborations.

Only a single-set one-act play, intended as part of a double bill, the dramatization condensed the sprawling incidents of the story into the period of a few hours: the late afternoon on which Butterfly believes her husband has come back to her and the early morning on which she realizes her mistake. The curtain was not lowered for the night-long vigil in between; this vigil, the most admired section of the play, was conveyed in one of the virtuosic light-and-sound montages of which Belasco was so fond. Here, as in many other moments of the play, William Furst's incidental music, based on authentic Japanese melodies, played an important part. Among the numerous plot changes from the story, the most vital is that in the play Butterfly actually kills herself instead of merely attempting to and then disappearing with Suzuki and the baby out of the clutches of the Americans.

The play had its successful premiere in New York on March 5, 1900, and a London production opened as early as April 28, 1900, running into July. The acclaimed star in London was the charming Evelyn Millard, who five years before had created the role of Cecily Cardew in *The Importance of Being Earnest*.

Puccini had arrived in London early in the summer to superintend the first Covent Garden production of his new opera *Tosca*, which had had its world premiere in Rome earlier that year. It is unclear whether Puccini went to see *Madame Butterfly* merely for amusement or whether he had been informed (perhaps even before leaving Italy) that it was a possible opera subject he could use. During the rest of 1900 he weighed its merits against those of other competing subjects, and decided in its favor by the end of the year. Negotiations with Belasco opened, and by the spring of 1901 were so far along that Puccini was able to send rough Italian translations of the story and the play to his regular librettist Luigi Illica (1857–1919), who had already done the Japanese opera *Iris* for Mascagni. As with the librettos of *Manon Lescaut* (1893), *La Bohème* (1896) and *Tosca*, Illica was now working together with the eminent playwright Giuseppe Giacosa (1847–1906), but Giacosa was already seriously ill and it is believed that his contribution to *Madama Butterfly* was small.

During the year 1902 the composer listened to records of Japanese music and had informative interviews with the great Japanese actress Sada Yacco and with the wife of the Japanese ambassador. But despite his impatience he did not receive the completion of the libretto until November of that year—and then decided to throw out one of the three acts, the one set in the American consulate (where two sections of the short story had taken place). In its final shape (that is, up to the opera's premiere), the libretto was in two acts, the second, longer one corresponding quite closely to Belasco's entire play, and the first one, with the wedding of Butterfly and Pinkerton, being substantially the librettists' invention, based on various suggestions from the story and play; the character of the bonze, for instance, had never existed before. The librettists allowed all the characters to express themselves in correct Italian, and the role of Butterfly, especially, was freed from most of its comic dross, making her the archetypical Puccini heroine crushed by the power of love.

The labor of composition was interrupted by a serious accident on February 25, 1903, when Puccini's car overturned and his leg was broken. He was unable to resume serious work until June and it was only on December 27 of that year that he completed the orchestration—with the Milan world premiere scheduled for the following February!

On January 3 of the new year, Puccini married Elvira Gemignani, who had left her husband for him some twenty years before. Now that her husband had died, the jealous and possessive woman could poison the rest of the amorous composer's days in an official capacity.

Although Puccini had great confidence in *Madama Butterfly* and the performers were excellent (conductor, Cleofonte Campanini; Butterfly, Rosina Storchio; Pinkerton, Giovanni Zenatello; Sharpless, Giuseppe De Luca), the La Scala premiere on February 17, 1904 was one of the greatest fiascos in opera history. The volatile, spoiled Milanese audience (which Puccini ironically called a *superpubblico*) thought they detected melodies carried over bodily from earlier Puccini operas, laughed when Storchio's dress accidentally billowed into a maternal swelling (they all knew about her liaison with Toscanini) and then roared when she actually produced little Trouble from the wings. When bird whistles were intentionally used in the orchestra to add to the atmosphere of the early-morning end of the vigil, the audience joined in enthusiastically. And so it went. Participation from the auditorium was so vociferous that some writers have suspected the existence of a cabal engineered by rivals of Puccini. But impatient dissatisfaction with the new music—aggravated by the hostility of critics who had been barred from rehearsals in a misguided attempt to create suspense—may have been a sufficient cause; after all, the La Scala productions of *Tosca* and *La Bohème* in 1900 had been coldly received.

Just as legendary as the Milan failure is the definitive triumph of *Madama Butterfly* only three months later, on May 28, 1904, at the more intimate Teatro Grande in Brescia—the high-water mark in that city's musical history. Brescia, where many friends of Puccini resided, had officially requested the honor of vindicating him. The Brescia Pinkerton was once again Zenatello, the Sharpless was the little-known Virgilio Bellatti, and the Butterfly was the Ukrainian soprano Salomea Kruszelnicka (Krusceniski in Italy), a highly dramatic singer capable of doing Wagner and Richard Strauss. Puccini had wanted the sweet, fluffy-voiced Storchio again but she had left on a South American tour with Toscanini, including *Butterfly* in her repertoire despite the Milan disaster.

As is well known, Puccini made some important changes in the opera for the Brescia production. The long second act was divided into two parts, with an intermission at the beginning of the vigil (the present volume uses "Act Two" and "Act Three," but these are still sometimes called the first and second parts of Act Two); "Addio, fiorito asil" was added to make Pinkerton's last-act appearance more tuneful; Trouble was no longer required to remain onstage from his first appearance straight through to the end of the vigil; the passage "Trionfa il mio amor" was added for Butterfly after the sighting of the ship; and about ten minutes was cut from the first act, especially introductions of relatives and a longish number for drunken Uncle Yakusidé.

It is not generally known, however, that the Brescia version—that is, the second version of 1904—was still quite different from the *Butterfly* normally given today. Puccini and his librettists continued making significant revisions through the end of 1906, especially for the first Paris production at the Opéra-Comique in December of that year. The definitive Italian-language vocal score (for voice and piano) was the fourth, issued in 1907, and it was not until that same year that a full orchestral score was published at all. That orchestral score, which differs in some verbal details from the vocal scores available today, has been used, with very slight modifications, as the source of the Italian text and punctuation in the present volume. It was also the source of the stage directions used here (very different at times from those in the vocal scores—but stage business will naturally vary from production to production, anyway); however, whereas the text in this volume is complete, the unusually voluminous original stage directions have been abridged and condensed by the translator, and appear here only in his own English phraseology.

Readers interested in such details will find in the Translator's Notes at the end of this volume (keyed to the libretto by numbers): brief descriptions of all but the most insignificant changes in the libretto made between the Brescia version (which so many people believe was the final one!) and the version normally done today; indications of loopholes in the plot and other anomalies remaining in the modern libretto as the result of cuts or oversights; and some information on Japanese culture as reflected (or distorted) in the libretto.

PLOT SUMMARY

ACT ONE

In the international port of Nagasaki, in the final years of the nineteenth century, Pinkerton, an American naval lieutenant, is renting a small house as a honeymoon cottage. Goro, who initiates him into the mysterious simplicity of a Japanese dwelling, has also acted as a marriage broker, arranging a very flexible contract for the convenience of a sailor on a limited tour of duty. The bride, however, takes the marriage very seriously: this is the warning of the American consul Sharpless, an understanding but very moralistic older man who now arrives as a guest at the impending wedding. Pinkerton, jovial but shallow and selfish, laughs this off. After the arrival of the excited fifteen-year-old bride, Butterfly, with her girl friends, Sharpless questions her and learns that her family is noble, but was impoverished by her father's death; she has been supporting her mother by working as a geisha. She keeps as a sacred relic the knife with which her father committed harakiri at the Emperor's command. In a quiet interlude she tells Pinkerton that out of love for him she has secretly converted to Christianity. Despite some comic wrangling among invited members of her family, the ceremony is successfully completed, but as toasts are being drunk, one of Butterfly's uncles, a bonze (Buddhist priest) makes an angry appearance, informs her family of her conversion and causes them to depart hastily, disowning her. When the married couple are alone at last, Butterfly's misgivings about her future are submerged in a trusting love for Pinkerton, and she yields to his ardor.

ACT TWO

Deserted for three years, penniless and now attended only by her faithful maid Suzuki, Butterfly is still confident that Pinkerton will return and that she has entered upon a binding American marriage. Thus, when the avaricious Goro brings the rich suitor Yamadori to call on her, she refuses to take the proposal seriously. Another visitor is Sharpless; he bears a letter from Pinkerton, whose return to Japan is indeed imminent but will be fraught with grief for Butterfly. Her excessive faith in her husband makes her overlook the words of warning and concentrate solely on the hints that he is returning. When Sharpless, "cruel, only to be kind," asks what she would do if Pinkerton never came back to her, she replies that she would return to the life of a geisha or, preferably, die. Angered by the consul's recommendation that she marry Yamadori, she shows him the child she gave birth to after Pinkerton's departure. Sharpless promises her he will inform Pinkerton of this development. After Sharpless leaves, Butterfly and Suzuki take Goro to task for spreading false rumors that the baby is illegitimate. When Goro escapes, the harbor cannon is heard signaling the arrival of a ship—Pinkerton's. Butterfly plans to await him in their home, dressed as on her bridal night. She and Suzuki decorate the house with flowers from the garden; then the two women and the child sit and wait for their lord and master.

ACT THREE

It is early the next morning. Butterfly, who has not slept a wink, is sent off by Suzuki, who now awakens, to get some rest. Pinkerton and Sharpless arrive to tell Suzuki that Pinkerton will never be back to stay. In fact, there is also an American woman with them—Pinkerton's legal wife, Kate. Now that the Pinkertons know about the baby, they wish to adopt him to better his lot. Pinkerton, a moral weakling, now feels remorse for his desertion but cannot stay to face Butterfly. Suzuki has intended to break matters slowly to her mistress in private, but Butterfly enters so hastily that she finds Sharpless and Kate still there, and soon knows the worst. Though giving up her child is a wrench she feels she cannot outlive, she says she must obey Pinkerton; she wants him to return in half an hour to claim the baby in person. Dismissing Suzuki, who guesses what is on her mind, Butterfly prepares to kill herself with her father's knife. Suzuki thrusts the child upon her in hopes of dissuading her, but this only delays the suicide. As Pinkerton and Sharpless return anxiously, Butterfly dies.

MADAMA BUTTERFLY

Opera in Three Acts
Music by Giacomo Puccini
Libretto by Luigi Illica
and Giuseppe Giacosa

CHARACTERS[1]*

MADAME BUTTERFLY (Cho-Cho-San)	Soprano
SUZUKI, her servant	Mezzo-Soprano
KATE PINKERTON	Mezzo-Soprano
B. F. PINKERTON, American naval lieutenant	Tenor
SHARPLESS, American consul at Nagasaki	Baritone
GORO, a marriage broker	Tenor
PRINCE YAMADORI	Baritone
THE BONZE, uncle of Cho-Cho-San	Bass
YAKUSIDÉ, another uncle	Bass
THE IMPERIAL COMMISSIONER	Bass
THE OFFICIAL REGISTRAR	Bass
CHO-CHO-SAN'S MOTHER	Mezzo-Soprano
CHO-CHO-SAN'S AUNT	Soprano
CHO-CHO-SAN'S COUSIN	Soprano
TROUBLE, Cho-Cho-San's child	
Wedding guests, servants	

* The small numbers refer throughout to the Translator's Notes at the end of the book.

xvi

ACT ONE

ACT ONE

Hill near Nagasaki.[2] *Japanese house, terrace and garden. In the background, below, the roadstead, harbor and city of Nagasaki.* GORO, *bowing and scraping, is showing the house to* PINKERTON, *sliding the partitions, etc. They move from the rooms upstage onto the terrace.*

PINKERTON *(surprised)*: ... E soffitto e pareti ...

GORO *(amused)*: Vanno e vengono a prova a norma che vi giova nello stesso locale alternar nuovi aspetti ai consueti.

PINKERTON *(in search of something)*: Il nido nuzial dov'è?

GORO *(pointing out two areas)*: Qui o là ... secondo ...

PINKERTON: Anch'esso a doppio fondo! La sala?

GORO *(showing the terrace)*: Ecco!

PINKERTON *(thunderstruck)*: All'aperto?

GORO *(closing a partition)*: Un fianco scorre ...

PINKERTON: Capisco! ... capisco! Un altro ...

PINKERTON *(surprised)*: ... And ceiling and walls ...

GORO *(amused)*: Come and go, back and forth, according to whether you want to give the same living space a new look or its old look.

PINKERTON *(in search of something)*: Where is the bridal chamber?

GORO *(pointing out two areas)*: Here or there ... depending ...

PINKERTON: That has a false bottom, too! The parlor?

GORO *(showing the terrace)*: Here it is!

PINKERTON *(thunderstruck)*: Outdoors?

GORO *(closing a partition)*: One side glides ...

PINKERTON: I understand! ... I understand! The other ...

3

GORO: Scivola!

PINKERTON: E la dimora frivola ...

GORO *(defensively)*: Salda come una torre da terra, fino al tetto.

PINKERTON: È una casa al sof-fietto.

GORO: Slides!

PINKERTON: And the whimsical domicile ...

GORO *(defensively)*: Solid as a tower from the ground up to the roof.

PINKERTON: The house folds up like an accordion!

They enter the garden. GORO *claps his hands three times. Two men and a woman* (SUZUKI) *enter and kneel to* PINKERTON *on the terrace.*

GORO: Questa è la cameriera che della vostra sposa fu già serva amorosa. Il cuoco ... il servi-tor. Son confusi del grande onore.

PINKERTON: I nomi?

GORO *(introducing them)*: Miss Nuvola leggera. Raggio di sol nascente. Esala aromi.[3]

SUZUKI *(still kneeling but embol-dened)*: Sorride Vostro Onore? Il riso è frutto e fiore. Disse il savio Ocunama: dei crucci la trama smaglia il sorriso. *(Entering the garden:)* Schiude alla perla il guscio, apre all'uomo l'uscio del Paradiso. Profumo degli Dei, Fontana della vita. Disse il savio Ocu-nama: dei crucci la trama sma-glia il sorriso.

GORO: This is the maid, who used to be your bride's loving servant. The cook ... the man-servant. They are embarrassed by the great honor.

PINKERTON: Their names?

GORO *(introducing them)*: Miss Light Cloud. Beam of the Rising Sun. Emitter of Good Smells.

SUZUKI *(still kneeling but embol-dened)*: Your Honor is smiling? Laughter is fruit and flower. The sage Okunama has said: "A smile unravels the web of woe. *(Entering the garden:)* It opens the shell to let the pearl appear; it throws open the gate of Paradise to man. Perfume of the gods, wellspring of life." The sage Okunama has said: "A smile unravels the web of woe."

GORO, *noticing that* PINKERTON *is getting bored with* SUZUKI'S *talkativeness, claps his hands. The three servants get up and escape quickly into the house.*

PINKERTON: A chiacchiere costei mi par cosmopolita. *(To* GORO, *who has moved upstage and is watching for something:)* Che guardi?

PINKERTON: As a chatterbox, she'd be at home all over the world! *(To* GORO, *who has moved upstage and is watching for something:)* What are you looking at?

GORO: Se non giunge ancor la sposa.

GORO: To see if the bride is coming yet.

PINKERTON: Tutto è pronto?

PINKERTON: Is everything ready?

GORO: Ogni cosa.

GORO: Every detail.

PINKERTON: Gran perla di sensale!

PINKERTON: You jewel of a marriage broker!

GORO *(with a deep bow of thanks)*: Qui verran: l'Ufficiale del registro, i parenti, il vostro Console, la fidanzata. Qui si firma l'atto e il matrimonio è fatto.

GORO *(with a deep bow of thanks)*: We're expecting: the official registrar, the relatives, your consul, your fiancée. The contract will be signed here and the wedding is over.

PINKERTON: E son molti i parenti?

PINKERTON: And are there a lot of relatives?

GORO: La suocera, la nonna,[4] lo zio Bonzo (che non ci degnerà di sua presenza) e cugini, e le cugine ... Mettiam fra gli ascendenti ... ed i collaterali, un due dozzine. Quanto alla discendenza ... *(Combining artfulness with humility:)* provederanno assai Vostra Grazia e la bella Butterfly.

GORO: Your mother-in-law, the grandmother, the uncle who's a bonze (he won't be honoring us with his presence) and male and female cousins ... Let's say, counting in the ascendant relatives ... and the collateral ones—about two dozen. As for the descendants ... *(Combining artfulness with humility:)* they will be well taken care of by

Your Honor and the lovely Butterfly.

PINKERTON: Gran perla di sensale!

PINKERTON: You jewel of a marriage broker!

They hear from a little distance the voice of SHARPLESS, *the consul, who is climbing the hill.*

SHARPLESS: E suda e arrampica! sbuffa, inciampica!

SHARPLESS: It's sweat and climb, puff and stumble!

GORO *(who has run upstage)*: Il Consol sale.

GORO *(who has run upstage)*: The Consul is coming up the hill.

SHARPLESS *enters puffing and* GORO *bows low before him.*

SHARPLESS: Ah!... quei ciottoli mi hanno sfiaccato!

SHARPLESS: Ah, those pebbles have worn me out!

PINKERTON *goes to meet him and they shake hands.*

PINKERTON: Bene arrivato.

PINKERTON: Welcome!

GORO: Bene arrivato.

GORO: Welcome!

SHARPLESS: Ouff!

SHARPLESS: Whew!

GORO: Presto, Goro, qualche ristoro.

PINKERTON: Quick, Goro, some refreshments.

GORO *enters the house hastily.*

SHARPLESS *(looking around)*: Alto.

SHARPLESS *(looking around)*: It's high up.

PINKERTON *(showing him the view)*: Ma bello!

PINKERTON *(showing him the view)*: But beautiful!

SHARPLESS *(studying the view)*: Nagasaki, il mare, il porto...

SHARPLESS *(studying the view)*: Nagasaki, the sea, the harbor ...

PINKERTON *(pointing to the house)*:
E una casetta che obbedisce a
bacchetta.

SHARPLESS: Vostra?

PINKERTON: La comperai per
novecentonovantanove anni,
con facoltà, ogni mese, di re-
scindere i patti.[5] Sono in questo
paese elastici del par, case e
contratti.

SHARPLESS: E l'uomo esperto ne
profitta.

PINKERTON: Certo.

PINKERTON *(pointing to the house)*:
And a little house that does
everything you tell it to!

SHARPLESS: Yours?

PINKERTON: I bought it for nine
hundred ninety-nine years,
with a monthly option of can-
celing the lease. In this country
the houses and the contracts
are equally flexible.

SHARPLESS: And a man of expe-
rience takes advantage of it.

PINKERTON: Of course.

Meanwhile GORO *has hurried out of the house followed by the two male
servants carrying glasses and bottles. The servants have gone back in
and* GORO *has prepared drinks. The two Americans take seats on the
terrace.*

PINKERTON *(with frankness)*: Do-
vunque al mondo lo Yankee
vagabondo si gode e traffica
sprezzando i rischi. Affonda
l'ancora alla ventura ...
(Pauses a moment to offer SHARP-
LESS *a drink:)* Milk-Punch o
Wisky? *(Resuming:)* Affonda
l'ancora alla ventura finchè
una raffica scompigli nave e or-
meggi, alberatura. La vita ei
non appaga se non fa suo tesor
i fiori d'ogni plaga, ...

PINKERTON *(with frankness)*: All
over the world, the roving
Yankee has a good time and
does business with no attention
to the risks involved. He drops
anchor as the spirit moves him
... *(Pauses a moment to offer*
SHARPLESS *a drink:)* Milk
punch or whiskey? *(Resuming:)*
He drops anchor as the spirit
moves him until one day a
squall pulls apart his ship with
its moorings and all the masts
and spars. He doesn't consider
his life complete if he doesn't
lay claim to the flowers of
every region, ...

SHARPLESS: È un facile vangelo ...

PINKERTON: ... d'ogni bella gli amor!

SHARPLESS: ... è un facile vangelo che fa la vita vaga ma che intristisce il cor.

PINKERTON: Vinto si tuffa, la sorte racciuffa. Il suo talento fa in ogni dove. Così mi sposo all'uso giapponese per novecentonovantanove anni. Salvo a proscioglermi ogni mese.

SHARPLESS: È un facile vangelo.

PINKERTON *(rising for the toast)*: America for ever!

SHARPLESS *(rising)*: America for ever! *(As they both sit:)* Ed è bella la sposa?

SHARPLESS: That's an easy code to live by ...

PINKERTON: ... to the love of every pretty woman!

SHARPLESS: ... that's an easy code to live by. It makes life amusing but it dries up your heart.

PINKERTON: If he's licked and goes under, he catches opportunity by the forelock again. He does just what he pleases wherever he is. And so I'm getting married Japanese style for nine hundred ninety-nine years. Free to liberate myself any month.

SHARPLESS: That's an easy code to live by.

PINKERTON *(rising for the toast)*: America forever!

SHARPLESS *(rising)*: America forever! *(As they both sit:)* And is the bride good-looking?

GORO, *who has heard this, comes forward officiously.*

GORO: Una ghirlanda di fiori freschi. Una stella dai raggi d'oro. E per nulla: sol cento yen. *(To* SHARPLESS:*)* Se Vostra Grazia mi comanda ce n'ho un assortimento.

GORO: A garland of fresh flowers. A star with golden beams. And for nothing: only a hundred yen. *(To* SHARPLESS:*)* If Your Honor will just say the word, I have an assortment of them.

SHARPLESS *laughs and declines. The Americans rise.*

PINKERTON *(with great impatience)*: Va, conducila, Goro.

PINKERTON *(with great impatience)*: Goro, go bring her!

GORO *runs upstage and exits, going down the hill.*

SHARPLESS: Quale smania vi prende? Sareste addirittura cotto?

SHARPLESS: What madness has taken hold of you? Are you really infatuated?

PINKERTON: Non so! ... non so! Dipende dal grado di cottura!⁶ Amore o grillo, dir non saprei. Certo costei m'ha coll'ingenue arti invescato. Lieve qual tenue vetro soffiato alla statura, al portamento sembra figura da paravento. Ma dal suo lucido fondo di lacca come con subito moto si stacca, qual farfalletta svolazza e posa con tal grazietta silenzïosa, che di rincorrerla furor m'assale ... se pure infrangerne dovessi l'ale.

PINKERTON: I don't know! ... I don't know! It depends on the degree of infatuation! Love or a caprice, I couldn't say. What is certain is that she's ensnared me with those naïve tricks of hers. As lightweight as the thinnest blown glass, in her size and her bearing she looks like a figure on a screen. But when she steps out of that shiny lacquer background with a sudden movement, like a little butterfly she flutters and alights with such a quiet charm that I'm in a frenzy to pursue her ... even if I should have to crush her wings.

SHARPLESS *(seriously though good-naturedly)*: Ier l'altro il Consolato sen' venne a visitar: io non la vidi, ma l'udii parlar. Di sua voce il mistero l'anima mi colpì. Certo quando è sincer l'amor parla così. ... Sarebbe gran peccato le lievi ali strappar e desolar forse un credulo cuor.

SHARPLESS *(seriously though good-naturedly)*: The other day she came to visit the consulate. I didn't see her but I heard her talk. The mystery in her voice touched my soul. Surely, that's the way love speaks when it's sincere. ... It would be a great pity to tear off those light wings and perhaps afflict a trusting heart.

PINKERTON: Console mio garbato, quetatevi, si sa ...

PINKERTON: My dear, good Consul, relax, everyone knows ...

SHARPLESS: Sarebbe gran peccato ...

SHARPLESS: It would be a great pity ...

PINKERTON: ... la vostra età è di flebile umor.

PINKERTON: ... that people of your age are a weepy bunch.

PINKERTON: Non c'è gran male s'io vo' quell'ale drizzare ai dolci voli dell'amor!

PINKERTON: There's no great harm if I want to direct those wings toward the sweet flights of love!

SHARPLESS: Quella divina mite vocina non dovrebbe dar note di dolor.

SHARPLESS: That divine, gentle little voice was not made to utter notes of sadness.

PINKERTON *(offering another drink)*: Wisky?

PINKERTON *(offering another drink)*: Whiskey?

SHARPLESS: Un altro bicchiere. *(After* PINKERTON *serves him and fills up his own glass, too:)* Bevo alla vostra famiglia lontana.

SHARPLESS: Another glass. *(After* PINKERTON *serves him and fills up his own glass, too:)* Here's to your family way back home.

PINKERTON *(raising his glass)*: E al giorno in cui mi sposerò con vere nozze, a una vera sposa americana.

PINKERTON *(raising his glass)*: And to the day when I get married at a real wedding to a real American bride!

GORO *reenters at a dash, coming from downhill.*

GORO: Ecco. Son giunte al sommo del pendìo. *(Points toward the path.)* Già del femmineo sciame qual di vento in fogliame s'ode il brusìo.

GORO: Here they are. They've arrived at the top of the slope. *(Points toward the path:)* Already you can hear the buzzing of the swarm of women like the sound of the wind rustling through leaves.

BUTTERFLY'S GIRL FRIENDS *(offstage)*: Ah! ah! ah!

BUTTERFLY'S GIRL FRIENDS *(offstage)*: Ah! ah! ah!

PINKERTON *and* SHARPLESS *move to the back of the garden and watch the path.*

GIRL FRIENDS *(still offstage)*: Ah! ah! ah! ah! Ah! Quanto cielo! Quanto mar! Quanto cielo! Quanto mar!

BUTTERFLY *(offstage)*: Ancora un passo or via.

GIRL FRIENDS: Come sei tarda!

BUTTERFLY: Aspetta.[7]

GIRL FRIENDS: Ecco la vetta. Guarda, guarda quanti fior!

BUTTERFLY: Spira sul mare e sulla terra —

GIRL FRIENDS: Quanto cielo! Quanto mar!

BUTTERFLY: — un primaveril soffio giocondo.

SHARPLESS: O allegro cinguettar di gioventù!

BUTTERFLY: Io sono la fanciulla più lieta del Giappone, —

GIRL FRIENDS: Quanti fior! Quanto mar!

BUTTERFLY: — anzi del mondo. Amiche, io son venuta —

GIRL FRIENDS: Quanto cielo! Quanto fior!

BUTTERFLY: — al richiamo d'amor, d'amor venni alle

GIRL FRIENDS *(still offstage)*: Ah! ah! ah! ah! Ah! All that sky! All that sea! All that sky! All that sea!

BUTTERFLY *(offstage)*: Come, just another step now.

GIRL FRIENDS: How slow you are!

BUTTERFLY: Wait.

GIRL FRIENDS: Here is the summit. Look, look at all those flowers!

BUTTERFLY: Blowing over the sea and over the land —

GIRL FRIENDS: All that sky! All that sea!

BUTTERFLY: — is a pleasant breath of springtime.

SHARPLESS: Oh, that merry chirping of youth!

BUTTERFLY: I'm the happiest girl in Japan, —

GIRL FRIENDS: All those flowers! All that sea!

BUTTERFLY: — no, in the world! Friends, I have come here —

GIRL FRIENDS: All that sky! All those flowers!

BUTTERFLY: — in answer to the call of love; I have come to the soglie ove s'accoglie il bene di chi vive e di chi muor!

GIRL FRIENDS (FIRST AND SECOND SOPRANOS): Gioia a te, gioia a te sia, dolce amica, ma pria di varcar la soglia che t'attira volgiti e mira, —

GIRL FRIENDS (THIRD SOPRANOS): Gioia a te, gioia a te sia, dolce amica, volgiti e mira le cose che ti son care, —

ALL THE GIRL FRIENDS: — mira quanto cielo, quanto fiori, quanto mar!...

BUTTERFLY: Amiche, io son venuta al richiamo d'amor, al richiamo d'amor, son venuta al richiamo d'amor [, d'amor]!*

GIRL FRIENDS (FIRST SOPRANOS): Gioia a te, gioia a te sia, dolce amica, ma pria di varcar la soglia volgiti, mira le cose che ti son care!

GIRL FRIENDS (SECOND AND THIRD SOPRANOS): Gioia a te, gioia a te sia, dolce amica, ma pria di varcar la soglia volgiti e guarda le cose che ti son sì care!

threshold of love, where the happiness of those who live and those who die is gathered!

GIRL FRIENDS (FIRST AND SECOND SOPRANOS): May you have joy, may you have joy, sweet friend, but before you cross the threshold that entices you, turn around and look, —

GIRL FRIENDS (THIRD SOPRANOS): May you have joy, may you have joy, sweet friend, turn around and look at the things that are dear to you, —

ALL THE GIRL FRIENDS: — look at all that sky, all those flowers, all that sea!...

BUTTERFLY: Friends, I have come here in answer to the call of love, the call of love, I have come in answer to the call of love [, of love]!

GIRL FRIENDS (FIRST SOPRANOS): May you have joy, may you have joy, sweet friend, but before you cross the threshold turn around, look at the things that are dear to you!

GIRL FRIENDS (SECOND AND THIRD SOPRANOS): May you have joy, may you have joy, sweet friend, but before you cross the threshold turn around and behold the things that are so dear to you!

* The bracketed text is omitted when the soprano elects to take the high D-flat.

BUTTERFLY *and her friends, having made it to the top of the hill, enter.*
All carry large open parasols, brightly colored.

BUTTERFLY: Siam giunte.	BUTTERFLY: We have arrived.

Seeing the three men, she recognizes PINKERTON. *She immediately closes her parasol and points him out to her friends.*

BUTTERFLY: B. F. Pinkerton. Giù! *(Kneels.)*	BUTTERFLY: B. F. Pinkerton. Down! *(Kneels.)*
GIRL FRIENDS *(closing parasols and kneeling)*: Giù!	GIRL FRIENDS *(closing parasols and kneeling)*: Down!

Then all rise and approach PINKERTON *ceremoniously.*

BUTTERFLY: Gran ventura.	BUTTERFLY: My great good fortune.
GIRL FRIENDS: Riverenza.	GIRL FRIENDS: Our humble respects.
PINKERTON *(smiling)*: È un po' dura la scalata?	PINKERTON *(smiling)*: The climb is a little hard?
BUTTERFLY: A una sposa costumata più penosa è l'impazienza ...	BUTTERFLY: To a well brought-up bride, impatience is more distressing ...
PINKERTON *(with slight mockery)*: Molto raro complimento.	PINKERTON *(with slight mockery)*: A very unusual compliment.
BUTTERFLY *(naïvely)*: Dei più belli ancor ne so.	BUTTERFLY *(naïvely)*: I know some much nicer ones.
PINKERTON *(following up quickly)*: Dei gioielli!	PINKERTON *(following up quickly)*: Real gems!
BUTTERFLY *(who wants to show off her stock of compliments)*: Se vi è caro sul momento ...	BUTTERFLY *(who wants to show off her stock of compliments)*: If you wish, right now ...
PINKERTON: Grazie, no.	PINKERTON: No, thanks.

SHARPLESS, *after observing the group of girls with curiosity, has approached* BUTTERFLY, *who listens to him attentively.*

SHARPLESS: Miss Butterfly. Bel nome, vi sta a meraviglia! Siete di Nagasaki?

SHARPLESS: Miss Butterfly. Lovely name, and it suits you perfectly! Are you from Nagasaki?

BUTTERFLY: Signor sì. Di famiglia assai prospera un tempo. *(To her friends:)* Verità?

BUTTERFLY: Yes, sir. Of a family that was once quite well-to-do. *(To her friends:)* True?

GIRL FRIENDS *(in eager agreement)*: Verità!

GIRL FRIENDS *(in eager agreement)*: True!

BUTTERFLY *(with perfect naturalness)*: Nessuno si confessa mai nato in povertà; non c'è vagabondo che a sentirlo non sia di gran prosapia. Eppur connobbi la ricchezza. Ma il turbine rovescia le quercie più robuste ... e abbiam fatto la ghescia[8] per sostentarci. *(To her friends:)* Vero?

BUTTERFLY *(with perfect naturalness)*: No one ever admits to having been born poor; there's no vagabond, to hear him tell it, who isn't of noble lineage. And yet I was acquainted with riches. But the whirlwind overturns the stoutest oaks ... and we served as geishas to keep ourselves alive. *(To her friends:)* True?

GIRL FRIENDS: Vero!

GIRL FRIENDS: True!

BUTTERFLY: Non lo nascondo, ne m'adonto. *(Noticing that* SHARPLESS *is smiling:)* Ridete? Perchè? Cose del mondo.

BUTTERFLY: I don't hide it and I'm not offended by it. *(Noticing that* SHARPLESS *is smiling:)* You're laughing? Why? That's how life is.

PINKERTON *(who has listened with interest, says in an aside to* SHARPLESS*)*: (Con quel fare di bambola quando parla m'infiamma.)

PINKERTON *(who has listened with interest, says in an aside to* SHARPLESS*)*: (When she talks that way and behaves like a doll, she sets me on fire.)

SHARPLESS *(to* BUTTERFLY*)*: E ci avete sorelle?

SHARPLESS *(to* BUTTERFLY*)*: And do you have any sisters?

BUTTERFLY: No signore. Ho la mamma.

BUTTERFLY: No, sir. I have my mother.

GORO *(pompously)*: Una nobile dama.

GORO *(pompously)*: A noble lady.

BUTTERFLY: Ma senza farle torto povera molto anch'essa.

BUTTERFLY: But—without wishing to belittle her—also very poor.

SHARPLESS: E vostro padre?

SHARPLESS: And your father?

BUTTERFLY *(taken aback, replies dryly after a pause)*: Morto.[9]

BUTTERFLY *(taken aback, replies dryly after a pause)*: Dead.

GORO *and the girl friends are embarrassed and fan themselves nervously.*

SHARPLESS: Quant'anni avete?

SHARPLESS: How old are you?

BUTTERFLY *(with almost childish coquettishness)*: Indovinate.

BUTTERFLY *(with almost childish coquettishness)*: Guess.

SHARPLESS: Dieci.

SHARPLESS: Ten.

BUTTERFLY: Crescete.

BUTTERFLY: Too low.

SHARPLESS: Venti.

SHARPLESS: Twenty.

BUTTERFLY: Calate. Quindici netti, netti; *(Artfully:)* sono vecchia diggià.

BUTTERFLY: Too high. Exactly fifteen. *(Artfully:)* I'm old by now.

SHARPLESS: Quindici anni!

SHARPLESS: Fifteen years old!

PINKERTON: Quindici anni!

PINKERTON: Fifteen years old!

SHARPLESS: L'età dei giuochi ...

SHARPLESS: The age for games ...

PINKERTON: — e dei confetti.[10]

PINKERTON: — and for candy.

GORO *(who sees more guests arriving)*: L'Imperial Commissario, l'Ufficiale del registro, i congiunti.

GORO *(who sees more guests arriving)*: The Imperial commissioner, the official registrar, the relatives.

PINKERTON *(to* GORO*)*: Fate presto.

PINKERTON *(to* GORO*)*: Move fast.

GORO *runs into the house.* BUTTERFLY *and her friends go to meet her relatives; ceremonious greetings are exchanged. The guests stare at the Americans.* GORO *takes the* COMMISSIONER *and* REGISTRAR *inside.* PINKERTON *takes* SHARPLESS *aside and speaks to him privately.*

PINKERTON: Che burletta la sfilata della nova parentela, tolta in prestito, a mesata!*

PINKERTON: What a comedy, this parade of my new relations, hired by the month!

4 SOPRANO GUESTS *(to* BUTTERFLY*)*: Dov'è?

4 SOPRANO GUESTS *(to* BUTTERFLY*)*: Where is he?

4 TENOR GUESTS: Dov'è?

4 TENOR GUESTS: Where is he?

BUTTERFLY AND 4 OTHER SOPRANO GUESTS: *(pointing to* PINKERTON*)*: Eccolo là!

BUTTERFLY AND 4 OTHER SOPRANO GUESTS *(pointing to* PINKERTON*)*: There he is over there!

PINKERTON: Certo dietro a quella vela di ventaglio pavonazzo, la mia suocera si cela.

PINKERTON: No doubt behind that purple canvas fan my mother-in-law is hiding.

A FEMALE COUSIN AND 4 TENOR GUESTS: Bello non è.

A FEMALE COUSIN AND 4 TENOR GUESTS: He's not good-looking.

4 TENOR GUESTS: Bello non è. In verità bello non è.

4 TENOR GUESTS: He's not good-looking. He's really not good-looking.

BUTTERFLY *(hurt)*: Bello è così che non si può ... sognar di più.

BUTTERFLY *(hurt)*: He's so good-looking that ... you couldn't dream of anyone more so.

OTHER GUESTS: Mi pare un re.

OTHER GUESTS: To me he's a king.

BUTTERFLY'S MOTHER: Mi pare un re!

BUTTERFLY'S MOTHER: To me he's a king!

OTHER GUESTS: Vale un Perù. Vale un Perù.

OTHER GUESTS: He's worth a fortune. He's worth a fortune.

* The following passage, printed in smaller type, is included in the definitive version of the score but often omitted in performance, creating an uncomfortable lack of balance and making the choral reprise unintelligible.

THE COUSIN *(to* BUTTERFLY*)*: Goro l'offrì pur anco a me.

BUTTERFLY *(with contempt)*: Sì, giusto tu!

PINKERTON *(pointing to* YAKUSIDÉ*)*: E quel coso da strapazzo è lo zio briaco e pazzo.[11]

VARIOUS GUESTS *(to the* COUSIN*)*: Ecco, perchè prescelta fu, vuol far con te la soprappiù.

OTHERS: La sua beltà già disfiorì.

FIRST GROUP: Divorzierà.

COUSIN AND VARIOUS GUESTS: Spero di sì.

OTHER GUESTS: Spero di sì.

OTHERS: La sua beltà già disfiorì.

GORO *(annoyed, to various guests)*: Per carità tacete un po' —

YAKUSIDÉ *(seeing servants bringing drinks)*: Vino ce n'è?

MOTHER AND AUNT *(casting sidelong glances)*: Guardiamo un po'.

SOME SOPRANO GUESTS *(to* YAKUSIDÉ*)*: Ne vidi già color di thè, color di thè, e chermisì!

OTHERS: La sua beltà già disfiorì, già disfiorì.

VARIOUS: Divorzierà.

MOTHER AND AUNT: Ah, hu! ah, hu!

FULL CHORUS: Ah, hu! Ah, hu! Ah, hu!

THE COUSIN *(to* BUTTERFLY*)*: Goro offered him to me as well.

BUTTERFLY *(with contempt)*: Yes, you of all people!

PINKERTON *(pointing to* YAKUSIDÉ*)*: And that no-good clown is the crazy, drunken uncle.

VARIOUS GUESTS *(to the* COUSIN*)*: That's it! Because she was the one chosen, she's trying to lord it over you.

OTHERS: Her beauty is already faded.

FIRST GROUP: She'll divorce.

COUSIN AND VARIOUS GUESTS: I hope so.

OTHER GUESTS: I hope so.

OTHERS: Her beauty is already faded.

GORO *(annoyed, to various guests)*: Please keep quiet —

YAKUSIDÉ *(seeing servants bringing drinks)*: Have they got wine?

MOTHER AND AUNT *(casting sidelong glances)*: Let's look and see.

SOME SOPRANO GUESTS *(to* YAKUSIDÉ*)*: I've already seen some that was the color of tea, the color of tea, and crimson!

OTHERS: Her beauty is already faded, already faded.

VARIOUS: She'll divorce.

MOTHER AND AUNT: Ah, hu! ah, hu!

FULL CHORUS: Ah, hu! Ah, hu! Ah, hu!

MOTHER: Mi pare un re. In verità bello è così che non si può sognar di più. Mi pare un re; bello è così che non si può sognar di più, sognar di più. Mi pare un re. Vale un Perù. Mi pare un re.

COUSIN: Goro l'offrì pur anco a me, ma s'ebbe un no! bello non è in verità. Goro l'offrì pur anco a me, ma s'ebbe un no. In verità bello non è, in verità. Divorzierà. Spero di sì. Divorzierà.

BUTTERFLY: Sì ... giusto tu!

AUNT: Vale un Perù. In verità bello è così che non si può sognar di più. Mi pare un re; bello è così che non si può sognar di più, sognar di più. Mi pare un re. Vale un Perù. Mi pare un re.

YAKUSIDÉ: Vino ce n'è? Guardiamo un po', guardiamo un po'. Ne vidi già color di thè, e chermisì, color di thè. Vino ce n'è? Vediamo un po'!

FIRST SOPRANO GUESTS: Bello non è, in verità, bello non è! bello non è, in verità. Goro l'offrì

MOTHER: To me he's a king. He really is so good-looking that you couldn't dream of anyone more so. To me he's a king; he's so good-looking that you couldn't dream of anyone more so, anyone more so. To me he's a king. He's worth a fortune. To me he's a king.

COUSIN: Goro offered him to me as well, but my answer was no! He's really not good-looking. Goro offered him to me as well, but my answer was no. He's really not good-looking, really not. She'll divorce. I hope so. She'll divorce.

BUTTERFLY: Yes ... you of all people!

AUNT: He's worth a fortune. He really is so good-looking that you couldn't dream of anyone more so. To me he's a king; he's so good-looking that you couldn't dream of anyone more so, anyone more so. To me he's a king. He's worth a fortune. To me he's a king.

YAKUSIDÉ: Have they got wine? Let's look and see, let's look and see. I've already seen some that was the color of tea, and crimson, the color of tea. Have they got wine? Let's see!

FIRST SOPRANO GUESTS: He's really not good-looking, he's not good-looking, he's really

pur anco a me, ma s'ebbe un no. In verità bello non è, in verità. Divorzierà. Spero di sì. Divorzierà!

SECOND SOPRANO GUESTS: Bello è così che non si può sognar di più! Mi pare un re. Vale un Perù! In verità è così bel che pare un re, in verità mi par un re, in verità. Divorzierà. Spero di sì. Divorzierà!

TENOR GUESTS: Bello non è, in verità, bello non è. Goro l'offrì pur anco a te, ma s'ebbe un no! ma s'ebbe un no! La sua beltà già disfiorì, già disfiorì. Divorzierà. Spero di sì. Divorzierà!

GORO: Per carità tacete un po' ... Sch! sch! sch!

SHARPLESS *(aside to* PINKERTON*)*: O amico fortunato!

SHARPLESS: O fortunato Pinkerton, che in sorte v'è toccato un fior pur or sbocciato!

PINKERTON: Sì, è vero, è un fiore, un fiore! L'esotico suo odore m'ha il cervello sconvolto.

COUSIN AND FIRST SOPRANOS: Ei

not good-looking. Goro offered him to me as well, but my answer was no. He's really not good-looking, really not. She'll divorce. I hope so. She'll divorce.

SECOND SOPRANO GUESTS: He's so good-looking that you couldn't dream of anyone more so. To me he's a king. He's worth a fortune! He really is so good-looking that to me he's a king, really to me he's a king, really. She'll divorce. I hope so. She'll divorce!

TENOR GUESTS: He's really not good-looking, he's not good-looking. Goro offered him to you as well, but your answer was no, but your answer was no! Her beauty is already faded, already faded. She'll divorce. I hope so. She'll divorce!

GORO: Please keep quiet! Sh! Sh! Sh!

SHARPLESS *(aside to* PINKERTON*)*: Oh, my fortunate friend!

SHARPLESS: Oh, fortunate Pinkerton, a flower just out of the bud has fallen to your lot!

PINKERTON: Yes, it's true, she's a flower, a flower! Her exotic fragrance has set my brain in a whirl.

COUSIN AND FIRST SOPRANOS: He

T

l'offrì pur anco a me! Ei l'offrì
pur anco a me! Ma risposi non
lo vo' e risposi: no!

offered him to me as well! He
offered him to me as well! But
I answered, "I don't want
him," and I answered no!

MOTHER AND SECOND SOPRANOS:
Egli è bel, mi pare un re! Egli
è bel, mi par un re! Non avrei
risposto no! non direi mai no!

MOTHER AND SECOND SOPRANOS:
He's good-looking, to me he's a
king! He's good-looking, to me
he's a king! I wouldn't have
answered no! I would never
say no!

SHARPLESS: Non più bella e
d'assai —

SHARPLESS: A more beautiful
girl, and I really mean it, —

SHARPLESS: — fanciulla io vidi
mai di questa Butterfly. E se a
voi sembran scede il patto e la
sua fede —

SHARPLESS: — than this Butterfly I have never seen! And if
you treat as jokes your contract
and her confidence —

PINKERTON: Sì, è vero, è un
fiore, un fiore, e in fede mia
l'ho colto!

PINKERTON: Yes, it's true, she's a
flower, a flower, and—on my
honor—I have picked it!

BUTTERFLY *(to her relatives)*:
Badate, attenti a me.

BUTTERFLY *(to her relatives)*:
Listen now, pay attention to
me.

COUSIN AND FIRST SOPRANOS:
Senza tanto ricercar io ne
trovo dei miglior, e gli dirò un
bel no, e gli dirò di no, di no!

COUSIN AND FIRST SOPRANOS:
Without looking too hard I'll
find better men, and I'll say
"Oh, no" to him, and I'll say
no to him, no!

MOTHER AND SECOND SOPRANOS:
No, mie care, non mi par, è
davvero un gran signor, nè gli
direi di no, nè mai direi di no,
di no!

MOTHER AND SECOND SOPRANOS:
No, my dear women, I dis-
agree, he's really a fine gentleman, and I wouldn't say no to
him, I would never say no, no!

TENORS: E divorzierà, e divorzierà, divorzierà!

TENORS: And she'll divorce, and
she'll divorce, she'll divorce!

SHARPLESS: — badate! ...
(Pointing to BUTTERFLY*:)* Ella ci
crede.

SHARPLESS: — look out! ...
(Pointing to BUTTERFLY*:)* She
believes in all this.

Meanwhile GORO *has collected the guests and has had the servants lay
out refreshments.*

BUTTERFLY *(to her* MOTHER*)*:
Mamma, vien qua. *(To the
other guests:)* Badate a me: attenti, orsù, *(In childish tones:)*
uno, due, tre e tutti giù.[12]

BUTTERFLY *(to her* MOTHER*)*:
Mother, come here. *(To the
other guests:)* Listen to me ...
pay attention ... now ... *(In
childish tones:)* one, two, three
and everybody down.

All the Japanese bow to PINKERTON *and* SHARPLESS.

PINKERTON *(separating* BUTTERFLY
from the rest): Vieni, amor mio!
Vi piace la casetta?

PINKERTON *(separating* BUTTERFLY
from the rest): Come, darling!
Do you like the little house?

BUTTERFLY *(showing her sleeves,
which are filled with objects)*:
Signor B. F. Pinkerton, perdo-
no ... Io vorrei ... pochi og-
getti da donna ...

BUTTERFLY *(showing her sleeves,
which are filled with objects)*: Mr.
B. F. Pinkerton, excuse me ...
I'd like to ... a few feminine
things ...

PINKERTON: Dove sono?

PINKERTON: Where are they?

BUTTERFLY: Sono qui ... vi di-
spiace?

BUTTERFLY: They're here ... are
you annoyed?

PINKERTON *(first smiles in surprise,
then gallantly gives permission)*: O
perchè mai, mia bella Butterfly?

PINKERTON *(first smiles in surprise,
then gallantly gives permission)*:
Why should I be, my lovely
Butterfly?

As she enumerates the items, she hands the contents of her sleeves to
SUZUKI, *who has come out, and who then takes them into the house.*

BUTTERFLY: Fazzoletti. La pipa. Una cintura. Un piccolo fermaglio. Uno specchio. Un ventaglio.

PINKERTON *(seeing a small container)*: Quel barattolo?

BUTTERFLY: Un vaso di tintura.

PINKERTON: Ohibò!

BUTTERFLY: Vi spiace? ... *(Throwing it away:)* Via!

PINKERTON *(seeing a long, narrow case)*: E quello?

BUTTERFLY *(very solemnly)*: Cosa sacra e mia.

PINKERTON: E non si può vedere?

BUTTERFLY: C'è troppa gente. Perdonate.

BUTTERFLY: Handkerchiefs. My pipe. A belt. A small brooch. A mirror. A fan.

PINKERTON *(seeing a small container)*: That little pot?

BUTTERFLY: A jar of hair dye.

PINKERTON: Tsk, tsk!

BUTTERFLY: You don't like it? ... *(Throwing it away:)* Out with it!

PINKERTON *(seeing a long, narrow case)*: And that?

BUTTERFLY *(very solemnly)*: A holy object that belongs to me.

PINKERTON: And can't it be shown?

BUTTERFLY: There are too many people around. Forgive me.

She takes the case into the house. GORO, *who has come near, whispers to* PINKERTON.

GORO: È un presente del Mikado a suo padre ... coll'invito *(Making a gesture indicative of harakiri)* ...

PINKERTON *(softly)*: E ... suo padre?

GORO: Ha obbedito.[13]

GORO: It was a present from the Mikado to her father ... with the invitation *(Making a gesture indicative of harakiri)* ...

PINKERTON *(softly)*: And ... her father?

GORO: Obeyed.

He rejoins the guests as BUTTERFLY *returns and takes some figurines from her sleeves.*

BUTTERFLY: Gli Ottokè.

PINKERTON (*examining one inquisitively*): Quei pupazzi? ... Avete detto?

BUTTERFLY: Son l'anime degli avi.

PINKERTON (*putting down the figurine*): Ah! il mio rispetto.

BUTTERFLY (*respectfully and trustingly*): Ieri son salita tutta sola in secreto alla Missione. Colla nuova mia vita posso adottare nuova religione. Lo zio Bonzo nol sa, nè i miei lo sanno. Io seguo il mio destino e piena d'umiltà al Dio del signor Pinkerton m'inchino. È mio destino. Nella stessa chiesetta in ginocchio con voi pregherò lo stesso Dio.[14] E per farvi contento potrò forse obliar la gente mia. Amore mio![15]

BUTTERFLY: The Ottokè.

PINKERTON (*examining one inquisitively*): Those puppets? ... What did you call them?

BUTTERFLY: They are the spirits of my ancestors.

PINKERTON (*putting down the figurine*): Oh! My respects.

BUTTERFLY (*respectfully and trustingly*): Yesterday I went up to the mission secretly, all by myself. Together with my new life I can also adopt a new religion. My uncle the bonze doesn't know about it, nor do my other relatives know. I am following my destiny, and full of humility I bow to the God of Mr. Pinkerton. It is my destiny. In the same church as you, kneeling beside you, I will pray to the same God. And to please you, perhaps I will be able to forget my own people. My love!

Meanwhile the ceremony is ready to begin, with the principals inside the house, which is revealed by opening a partition.

GORO: Tutti zitti!

COMMISSIONER (*reading from the marriage contract*): È concesso al nominato Benjamin Franklin Pinkerton, Luogotenente nella cannoniera *Lincoln*,[16] marina degli Stati Uniti, America del

GORO: Everyone quiet!

COMMISSIONER (*reading from the marriage contract*): It is granted to the man by the name of Benjamin Franklin Pinkerton, lieutenant on the gunboat *Lincoln* of the navy of the United

Nord: ed alla damigella Butterfly del quartiere d'Omara-Nagasaki, d'unirsi in matrimonio, per dritto il primo, della propria volontà, ed ella per consenso[17] dei parenti qui testimonî all'atto. *(Hands the contract to be signed.)*

States, North America; and to the young woman Butterfly of the quarter of Omara, Nagasaki, to join in matrimony; the former by virtue of his own will, and the latter by consent of her relations who are here as witnesses to the ceremony. *(Hands the contract to be signed.)*

GORO *(ceremoniously)*: Lo sposo. Poi la sposa. *(They sign.)* E tutto è fatto.

GORO *(ceremoniously)*: The groom. Then the bride. *(They sign.)* And it's all done.

The guests come to congratulate BUTTERFLY.

GIRL FRIENDS: Madama Butterfly!

GIRL FRIENDS: Madame Butterfly!

BUTTERFLY *(correcting them)*: Madama B. F. Pinkerton.

BUTTERFLY *(correcting them)*: Mrs. B. F. Pinkerton.

The REGISTRAR *collects the papers and informs the* COMMISSIONER *that the ceremony is over.*

COMMISSIONER *(taking leave of* PINKERTON*)*: Augurî molti.

COMMISSIONER *(taking leave of* PINKERTON*)*: Best wishes.

PINKERTON: I miei ringraziamenti.

PINKERTON: My thanks.

COMMISSIONER *(to* SHARPLESS*)*: Il signor Console scende?

COMMISSIONER *(to* SHARPLESS*)*: Are you coming down, Consul?

SHARPLESS: L'accompagno. *(To* PINKERTON:*)* Ci vedrem domani.

SHARPLESS: I'll go with you. *(To* PINKERTON:*)* We'll meet tomorrow.

PINKERTON: A meraviglia.

PINKERTON: Fine!

REGISTRAR *(taking leave of* PINKERTON*)*: Posterità.

REGISTRAR *(taking leave of* PINKERTON*)*: May it be a fruitful marriage.

PINKERTON: Mi proverò.   PINKERTON: I'll try.

SHARPLESS *leaves with the other officials, but returns for a last word to*
PINKERTON.

SHARPLESS: Giudizio!   SHARPLESS: Act wisely!

PINKERTON *waves to him reassuringly as he goes. The servants distribute drinks.*

PINKERTON *(to himself)*: (Ed eccoci in famiglia. Sbrighiamoci al più presto in modo onesto.)[18] *(Aloud, toasting:)* Hip! Hip!

PINKERTON *(to himself)*: (And here we are in the bosom of our family. Let's get out of this as fast as conventions will allow!) *(Aloud, toasting:)* Hip! Hip!

SOPRANO GUESTS: O Kami! O Kami!

SOPRANO GUESTS: Oh, Kami! Oh, Kami!

PINKERTON: Beviamo ai novissimi legami, —

PINKERTON: Let's drink to our brand-new relationship, —

YAKUSIDÉ AND TENORS: O Kami! O Kami!

YAKUSIDÉ AND TENORS: Oh, Kami! Oh, Kami!

PINKERTON: — beviamo ai novissimi legami.

PINKERTON: — let's drink to our brand-new relationship!

COUSIN AND MOTHER: Beviamo, beviamo.

COUSIN AND MOTHER: Let's drink, let's drink!

COUSIN, MOTHER, SOPRANOS: O Kami! O Kami! Beviamo ai novissimi legami.

COUSIN, MOTHER, SOPRANOS: Oh, Kami! Oh, Kami! Let's drink to our brand-new relationship!

BONZE *(offstage)*: Cio-cio-san! Cio-cio-san! Abbominazione!

BONZE *(offstage)*: Cho-Cho-San! Cho-Cho-San! Abomination!

GUESTS *(huddled together in shock)*, BUTTERFLY: Lo zio Bonzo!

GUESTS *(huddled together in shock)*, BUTTERFLY: The bonze! Her [My] uncle!

{ GORO: Un corno al guastafeste! Chi ci leva d'intorno le persone moleste?!...

{ GORO: Darn the spoilsport! Who'll rid us of unwanted people?!...

BONZE *(offstage)*: Cio-cio-san! Cio-cio-san!

BONZE: Cio-cio-san! *(Entering in a fury, with some attendants:)* Cio-cio-san! *(Threateningly, to* BUTTERFLY:*)* Che hai tu fatto alla Missione?

COUSIN AND OTHER GUESTS: Rispondi, Cio-cio-san!

PINKERTON *(angrily)*: Che mi strilla quel matto?

BONZE: Rispondi, che hai tu fatto?

GUESTS: Rispondi, Cio-cio-san!

BONZE: Come, hai tu gli occhi asciutti? Son dunque questi i frutti? *(Roaring:)* Ci ha rinnegato tutti!

GUESTS: Hou! Cio-cio-san!

BONZE: Rinnegato, vi dico, il culto antico —

GUESTS: Hou! Cio-cio-san!

BONZE *(offstage)*: Cho-Cho-San! Cho-Cho-San!

BONZE: Cho-Cho-San! *(Entering in a fury, with some attendants:)* Cho-Cho-San! *(Threateningly, to* BUTTERFLY:*)* What did you do at the mission?

COUSIN AND OTHER GUESTS: Answer, Cho-Cho-San!

PINKERTON *(angrily)*: What is that lunatic shrieking about?

BONZE: Answer: what did you do?

GUESTS: Answer, Cho-Cho-San!

BONZE: What! Your eyes are dry? So this is where it leads! *(Roaring:)* She has renounced us all!

GUESTS: Hou! Cho-Cho-San!

BONZE: Renounced, I tell you, the ancient religion —

GUESTS: Hou! Cho-Cho-San!

The BONZE *pushes aside the* MOTHER *as she tries to defend* BUTTERFLY, *who has hidden her face in her hands.*

BONZE: Kami[19] Sarundasico!

GUESTS: Hou! Cio-cio-san!

BONZE: All'anima tua guasta qual supplizio sovrasta!

PINKERTON *(intervening impatiently)*: Ehi, dico: basta, basta!

BONZE: Kami Sarundasico!

GUESTS: Hou! Cho-Cho-San!

BONZE: What torment awaits your tainted soul!

PINKERTON *(intervening impatiently)*: Hey, listen! That's enough! Enough!

The BONZE *stops short for a moment, then resolutely urges the guests to leave.*

BONZE: Venite tutti. Andiamo! *(To* BUTTERFLY:*)* Ci hai rinnegato e noi ...

BONZE, YAKUSIDÉ, GUESTS: Ti rinneghiamo!

PINKERTON *(in a tone of command)*: Sbarazzate all'istante. In casa mia niente baccano e niente bonzeria.

GUESTS *(rushing away, taking along the* MOTHER*)*: Hou! Hou! Cio-cio-san! Hou! Cio-cio-san!

BONZE, YAKUSIDÉ, TENORS *(offstage, their voices growing fainter)*: Kami Sarundasico!

SOPRANO GUESTS: Hou! Cio-cio-san!

BONZE, YAKUSIDÉ, TENORS: Ti rinneghiamo!

SOPRANO GUESTS: Hou! Cio-cio-san!

BONZE, YAKUSIDÉ, ALL GUESTS: Ti rinneghiamo!

ALL GUESTS: Hou! Cio-cio-san!

SOPRANO GUESTS: Hou! Cio-cio-san!

BONZE: Everybody, come! We're leaving! *(To* BUTTERFLY:*)* You have renounced us and we ...

BONZE, YAKUSIDÉ, GUESTS: — disown you!

PINKERTON *(in a tone of command)*: Get out of here at once! In my house I'll have no uproar and no priest's antics!

GUESTS *(rushing away, taking along the* MOTHER*)*: Hou! Hou! Cho-Cho-San! Hou! Cho-Cho-San!

BONZE, YAKUSIDÉ, TENORS *(offstage, their voices growing fainter)*: Kami Sarundasico!

SOPRANO GUESTS: Hou! Cho-Cho-San!

BONZE, YAKUSIDÉ, TENORS: We disown you!

SOPRANO GUESTS: Hou! Cho-Cho-San!

BONZE, YAKUSIDÉ, ALL GUESTS: We disown you!

ALL GUESTS: Hou! Cho-Cho-San!

SOPRANO GUESTS: Hou! Cho-Cho-San!

BUTTERFLY *bursts into childish tears.* PINKERTON *comes to her aid and takes her hands from her face.*

PINKERTON: Bimba, bimba, non piangere per gracchiar di ranocchi ...

SOPRANO GUESTS *(very far off)*: Hou! Cio-cio-san!

BUTTERFLY *(holding her ears)*: Urlano ancor!

PINKERTON *(reassuringly)*: Tutta la tua tribù e i Bonzi tutti del Giappon non valgono il pianto di quegli occhi cari e belli.

BUTTERFLY *(with a childlike smile)*: Davver? Non piango più. E quasi del ripudio non mi duole per le vostre parole che mi suonan così dolci nel cor. *(Starts to kiss his hand.)*

PINKERTON *(stopping her gently)*: Che fai? ... la man?

BUTTERFLY: Mi han detto che laggiù fra la gente costumata è questo il segno del maggior rispetto.

SUZUKI *(from inside, muttering)*: E Izaghi ed Izanami Sarundasico, e Kami, e Izaghi ed Izanami Sarundasico, e Kami.

PINKERTON *(in surprise)*: Chi brontola lassù?

BUTTERFLY: È Suzuki che fa la sua preghiera seral.

PINKERTON: Child, child, don't cry over the croaking of frogs ...

SOPRANO GUESTS *(very far off)*: Hou! Cho-Cho-San!

BUTTERFLY *(holding her ears)*: They're still howling!

PINKERTON *(reassuringly)*: Your whole tribe and all the bonzes in Japan aren't worth the tears of those dear, beautiful eyes.

BUTTERFLY *(with a childlike smile)*: Really? I won't cry any more. And I've almost gotten over being renounced, thanks to your words that ring so sweetly in my heart. *(Starts to kiss his hand.)*

PINKERTON *(stopping her gently)*: What are you doing? My hand?

BUTTERFLY: I've been told that in your country, among well-mannered people, that is the sign of the greatest respect.

SUZUKI *(from inside, muttering)*: And Izagi and Izanami Sarundasico, and Kami, and Izagi and Izanami Sarundasico, and Kami.

PINKERTON *(in surprise)*: Who's muttering up there?

BUTTERFLY: It's Suzuki reciting her evening prayer.

PINKERTON (*drawing her toward the house*): Viene la sera —

PINKERTON (*drawing her toward the house*): Evening is falling —

BUTTERFLY: ... e l'ombra e la quiete.

BUTTERFLY: ... and all is dark and peaceful.

PINKERTON: E sei qui sola —

PINKERTON: And you are here alone —

BUTTERFLY: Sola e rinnegata! Rinnegata! e felice!

BUTTERFLY: Alone and disowned! Disowned—and happy!

PINKERTON *claps for the servants, who all enter.*

PINKERTON: A voi, chiudete.

PINKERTON: You there, close the partitions!

The male servants close the partitions, creating a room alongside the terrace, and eventually leave.

BUTTERFLY: Sì, sì, noi tutti soli ... E fuori il mondo ...

BUTTERFLY: Yes, yes, just us all alone ... and the world locked out ...

PINKERTON (*laughing*): E il Bonzo furibondo.

PINKERTON (*laughing*): And the furious bonze.

BUTTERFLY: Suzuki, le mie vesti.

BUTTERFLY: Suzuki, my robes.

SUZUKI *finds nightwear and toilet articles in a chest.*

SUZUKI (*bowing to* PINKERTON): Buona notte.

SUZUKI (*bowing to* PINKERTON): Good night.

BUTTERFLY, *in the house, changes her wedding dress for a white robe, then sits down with a small mirror to arrange her hair as* SUZUKI *leaves.* PINKERTON *watches his bride lovingly.*

BUTTERFLY: Quest'obi[20] pomposa di scioglier mi tarda ...

BUTTERFLY: I can't wait to take off this fancy robe ...

PINKERTON: Con moti di scojattolo i nodi allenta e scioglie! ... Pensar che quel giocattolo è mia moglie! mia moglie! Ma tal grazia dispiega, ch'io mi struggo per la febbre d'un subito desio.

BUTTERFLY: — si vesta la sposa di puro candor. Tra motti sommessi sorride e mi guarda. Celarmi potessi! ne ho tanto rossor! E ancor l'irata voce mi maledice ...

PINKERTON: With movements like a squirrel's she loosens and opens the bows! ... To think that that toy is my wife! My wife! But she displays such grace that I am consumed by the fever of a sudden desire.

BUTTERFLY: — let the bride be dressed in purest white. With murmured comments he is smiling and watching me. I wish I could hide! It embarrasses me so! And still I can hear that angry voice cursing me ...

BUTTERFLY *(as he approaches her)*: — Butterfly, rinnegata ... Rinnegata ... e felice ...

BUTTERFLY *(as he approaches her)*: — Butterfly, disowned ... Disowned—and happy ...

PINKERTON *(leading her onto the terrace)*: Bimba dagli occhi pieni di malia, ora sei tutta mia. Sei tutta vestita di giglio. Mi piace la treccia tua bruna fra i candidi veli.

PINKERTON *(leading her onto the terrace)*: Child with eyes full of enchantment, now you are all mine. You are all in white like a lily. I like your dark hair against the white garments.

BUTTERFLY *(stepping down from the terrace)*: Somiglio la Dea della luna, la piccola Dea della luna che scende la notte dal ponte del ciel.

BUTTERFLY *(stepping down from the terrace)*: I am like the goddess of the moon, the little goddess of the moon who descends at night from the bridge of heaven.

PINKERTON: E affascina i cuori ...

PINKERTON: And casts a spell over people's hearts ...

BUTTERFLY: E li prende, e li avvolge in un bianco mantel — E via se li reca negli alti reami.

BUTTERFLY: And takes them and envelops them in a white mantle — And carries them off into the lofty realms.

PINKERTON: Ma intanto finor non m'hai detto, ancor non m'hai detto che m'ami. Le sa quella Dea le parole che appagan gli ardenti desir?

BUTTERFLY: Le sa. Forse dirle non vuole per tema d'averne a morir, per tema d'averne a morir!

PINKERTON: Stolta paura, l'amor non uccide, ma dà vita, e sorride per gioie celestiali come ora fa nei tuoi lunghi occhi ovali.[21] *(Caressing her face.)*

BUTTERFLY *(pulling away)*: Adesso voi siete per me l'occhio del firmamento. E mi piaceste dal primo momento che vi ho veduto.

PINKERTON: But in the meantime you haven't told me yet, you still haven't told me that you love me. Does that goddess know the words that quench ardent desires?

BUTTERFLY: She knows them. Perhaps she doesn't want to say them for fear she will have to die of it, for fear she will have to die of it!

PINKERTON: A foolish fear: love doesn't kill, but gives life, and smiles for celestial joys, as it is now doing in your long oval eyes.

BUTTERFLY *(pulling away)*: Now you are for me the eye of heaven. And I liked you from the moment I first saw you.

For a moment she starts, seeming to hear her relatives' curse, then she recovers.

BUTTERFLY: Siete alto, forte. Ridete con modi sì palesi e dite cose che mai non intesi. Or son contenta, or son contenta. *(Kneeling at his feet:)* Vogliatemi bene, un bene piccolino, un bene da bambino, quale a me si conviene. Vogliatemi bene. Noi siamo gente avvezza alle piccole cose umili e silenziose, ad una tenerezza sfiorante e pur profonda come il ciel, come l'onda del mare!

BUTTERFLY: You are tall, strong. You laugh in such a forthright way and you say things that I never heard. Now I am contented, now I am contented. *(Kneeling at his feet:)* Love me, just a little bit, the way you would love a child; that's the kind of love fitting for me. Love me. We Japanese are people accustomed to the little things, humble and quiet things, to a tenderness that

PINKERTON: Dammi ch'io baci le tue mani care. Mia Butterfly! come t'han ben nomata tenue farfalla ...

BUTTERFLY *(pulling her hands away, sadly)*: Dicon che oltre mare se cade in man dell'uom, ogni farfalla da uno spillo è trafitta ed in tavola infitta!

PINKERTON *(smiling, taking her hands again)*: Un po' di vero c'è. E tu lo sai perchè? Perchè non fugga piu. *(Embracing her:)* Io t'ho ghermita. Ti serro palpitante. Sei mia.

BUTTERFLY *(now totally unresisting)*: Sì, per la vita.

PINKERTON: Vieni, vieni! Via dall'anima in pena l'angoscia paurosa. *(Pointing to the sky, in which the stars have appeared:)* È notte serena! Guarda: dorme ogni cosa!

BUTTERFLY *(in rapture)*: Ah! Dolce notte!

PINKERTON: Vieni, vieni! ...

BUTTERFLY: Quante stelle!

touches ever so lightly and yet is as deep as the sky is high, as deep as the waves of the sea!

PINKERTON: Give me your dear hands to kiss. My Butterfly! How well they named you, fragile butterfly ...

BUTTERFLY *(pulling her hands away, sadly)*: They say that across the sea every butterfly that falls into the hands of a man is pierced with a pin and stuck onto a board!

PINKERTON *(smiling, taking her hands again)*: There is some truth to that. And you know why? So it can't escape again. *(Embracing her:)* I have caught you. I press your quivering body close to me. You are mine.

BUTTERFLY *(now totally unresisting)*: Yes, for life!

PINKERTON: Come! Come! No more fearful anguish in your tortured soul! *(Pointing to the sky, in which the stars have appeared:)* It's a clear, starry night! Look: everything is asleep!

BUTTERFLY *(in rapture)*: Ah! Sweet night!

PINKERTON: Come! Come!

BUTTERFLY: So many stars!

BUTTERFLY: Non le vidi mai sì belle!

PINKERTON: È notte serena!

PINKERTON: Ah! vieni, vieni! È notte serena! Guarda: dorme ogni cosa!

BUTTERFLY: Dolce notte! Quante stelle!

PINKERTON: Vieni, vieni! —

BUTTERFLY: Non le vidi mai sì belle!

PINKERTON: — vieni, vieni!

BUTTERFLY: Trema, brilla ogni favilla *(As fireflies appear all around)* —

PINKERTON: Vien, sei mia!...

BUTTERFLY: — col baglior d'una pupilla.

PINKERTON: Via l'angoscia dal tuo cor — Ti serro palpitante. Sei mia. Ah, vien, vien, sei mia! Ah! Vieni, guarda: dorme ogni cosa!

BUTTERFLY: Oh! Oh! quanti occhi fissi, attenti d'ogni parte a riguardar! pei firmamenti, via pei lidi, via pel mare!

BUTTERFLY: I've never seen them look so beautiful!

PINKERTON: It's a clear, starry night!

PINKERTON: Ah, come! Come! It's a clear, starry night! Look: everything is asleep!

BUTTERFLY: Sweet night! So many stars!

PINKERTON: Come! Come!

BUTTERFLY: I've never seen them look so beautiful!

PINKERTON: Come! Come!

BUTTERFLY: Every spark of light is trembling, shining *(As fireflies appear all around)* —

PINKERTON: Come! You are mine!...

BUTTERFLY: — with a glow like that of human eyes.

PINKERTON: No more anguish in your heart — I press your quivering body close to me. You are mine. Ah, come! Come! You are mine! Ah! Come, look: everything is asleep!

BUTTERFLY: Oh! Oh! So many motionless eyes watching closely everywhere! In the heavens, out over the shore, out over the sea!

PINKERTON: Ti serro palpitante. Ah, vien! ...

PINKERTON: I press your quivering body close to me. Ah, come! ...

BUTTERFLY: Oh! quanti occhi fissi, attenti!

BUTTERFLY: Oh! So many motionless eyes watching!

{
BUTTERFLY: Quanti sguardi — ride il ciel! Ah! Dolce notte! Tutto estatico d'amor ride il ciel!

PINKERTON: Guarda: dorme ogni cosa. Ah! vien! Ah! vieni, vieni! ... Ah! vien, ah! vien! [sei mia!]*
}

{
BUTTERFLY: So many onlookers — The sky is laughing! Ah! Sweet night! All ecstatic with love, the sky is laughing!

PINKERTON: Look: everything is asleep. Ah, come! Ah, come! Come! ... Ah, come! Ah, come! [You are mine!]
}

They enter the house.

---

* The last two words are omitted if the tenor elects to take the high C.

ACT TWO

ACT TWO

Inside BUTTERFLY'S *house, which is dark, with all the partitions closed.* SUZUKI *is curled up in prayer before an image of Buddha, ringing the prayer hand-bell from time to time, while* BUTTERFLY *lies on the floor, resting her head in her hands.*

SUZUKI: E Izaghi ed Izanami, Sarundasico e Kami ... *(Breaking off:)* Oh! la mia testa! *(Ringing:)* E tu Ten-Sjo-o-daj! fate che Butterfly non pianga più, mai più! mai più!

BUTTERFLY: Pigri ed obesi son gli Dei giapponesi. L'americano Iddio son persuasa ben più presto risponde a chi l'implori. Ma temo ch'egli ignori che noi stiam qui di casa.

SUZUKI: And Izagi and Izanami, Sarundasico and Kami ... *(Breaking off:)* Oh, my head! *(Ringing:)* And you, Ten-sho-o-dai! Bring it about that Butterfly shall never cry again, never again, never again!

BUTTERFLY: The Japanese gods are lazy and fat. The American God, I'm convinced, replies much more quickly to those who supplicate him. But I'm afraid he doesn't know we live here.

SUZUKI *has opened the partition upstage leading to the garden.*

BUTTERFLY: Suzuki, è lungi la miseria?

SUZUKI *(taking some coins from a small chest)*: Questo è l'ultimo fondo.

BUTTERFLY: Questo? Oh! troppe spese!

BUTTERFLY: Suzuki, is poverty far off?

SUZUKI *(taking some coins from a small chest)*: This is our last capital.

BUTTERFLY: This! Oh, we've spent too much!

SUZUKI (*putting back the money*): S'egli non torna e presto, siamo male in arnese.

BUTTERFLY (*resolutely*): Ma torna.

SUZUKI (*shaking her head*): Tornera!

BUTTERFLY (*annoyed*): Perchè dispone che il Console provveda alla pigione, rispondi su! Perchè con tante cure la casa rifornì di serrature, s'ei non volesse ritornar mai più?

SUZUKI: Non lo so.

BUTTERFLY: Non lo sai? (*Proudly:*) Io te lo dico. Per tener ben fuori le zanzare, i parenti ed i dolori, e dentro, con gelosa custodia, la sua sposa, la sua sposa che son io, Butterfly.

SUZUKI (*unconvinced*): Mai non s'è udito di straniero marito che sia tornato al suo nido.

BUTTERFLY (*in a fury*): Ah! Taci! o t'uccido. (*Persuasively:*) Quell'ultima mattina: tornerete, signor? gli domandai. Egli, col cuore grosso, per celarmi la pena ... sorridendo rispose: O Butterfly ... piccina mogliettina, tornerò colle rose alla stagione serena quando fa la nidiata il pettirosso.[22] (*With conviction:*) Tornerà.

SUZUKI (*putting back the money*): If he doesn't return, and quickly, we'll be in a bad way.

BUTTERFLY (*resolutely*): But he *is* returning.

SUZUKI (*shaking her head*): He'll return!

BUTTERFLY (*annoyed*): Why does he arrange for the Consul to pay the rent? Answer me, come on! Why did he so carefully have locks installed in the house if he didn't intend ever to return?

SUZUKI: I don't know.

BUTTERFLY: You don't know? (*Proudly:*) I'll tell you. To keep out mosquitos, relatives and troubles, and ~to keep in— jealously guarded—his wife, his wife—me, Butterfly.

SUZUKI (*unconvinced*): No one ever heard of a foreign husband coming back to his home.

BUTTERFLY (*in a fury*): Ah! Keep quiet or I'll kill you! (*Persuasively:*) That last morning — "Will you come back, sir?" I asked him. He, with a heavy heart, in order to conceal his sorrow from me, smiled and answered: "Oh, Butterfly, my tiny little wife, I'll come back with the roses in the mild season when the robin makes

its nest." *(With conviction:)* He will return.

SUZUKI *(unbelieving):* Speriam.

SUZUKI *(unbelieving):* Let's hope so.

BUTTERFLY *(insisting):* Dillo con me. Tornerà.

BUTTERFLY *(insisting):* Repeat after me: he will return.

SUZUKI *(to please her):* Tornerà ... *(Starts to cry.)*

SUZUKI *(to please her):* He will return ... *(Starts to cry.)*

BUTTERFLY *(surprised):* Piangi? Perchè? perchè? Ah, la fede ti manca ... *(Confidently, smiling:)* Senti. *(Acting out the incidents she describes:)* Un bel dì, vedremo levarsi un fil di fumo dall'estremo²³ confin del mare. E poi la nave appare. Poi la nave bianca entra nel porto, romba il suo saluto. Vedi? È venuto! Io non gli scendo incontro. Io no. Mi metto là sul ciglio del colle e aspetto, e aspetto gran tempo e non mi pesa la lunga attesa. E uscito dalla folla cittadina un uomo, un picciol punto s'avvia per la collina ... Chi sarà? chi sarà? E come sarà giunto che dirà? che dirà? Chiamerà Butterfly dalla lontana. Io senza dar risposta me ne starò nascosta un po' per celia ... e un po' per non morire al primo incontro, ed egli alquanto in pena chiamerà, chiamerà: Piccina mogliettina olezzo di verbena, i nomi che mi dava al suo venire — Tutto questo avverrà, te lo

BUTTERFLY *(surprised):* You're crying? Why? Why? Ah, you are lacking in faith ... *(Confidently, smiling:)* Listen. *(Acting out the incidents she describes:)* One fine day, we will see a wisp of smoke rising at the furthest edge of the sea. And then the ship will appear. Then the white ship will enter the harbor and fire its gun in salute. Do you see? He has come! I won't go down to meet him. Not me. I'll station myself there on the rim of the hill and I'll wait, and I'll wait a long time, and the long wait won't bother me. And, emerging from the city's crowd, a man, a tiny dot, will make his way up the hill ... Who will it be? Who will it be? And, when he arrives, what will he say? What will he say? He will call "Butterfly" from the distance. I will make no answer but will keep hidden, partly as a joke ... and partly so I won't die at our first meeting. And he, a

prometto. Tienti la tua paura, io con sicura fede l'aspetto.

little worried, will call, will call: "Tiny little wife, fragrance of verbena"—the names he used to call me when he arrived. All this will happen, I promise you. You can keep your fears. As for me, I await him with unshaken faith.

They embrace. BUTTERFLY *dismisses* SUZUKI, *who exits left.* GORO *and* SHARPLESS *appear in the garden.*

GORO *(looking in)*: C'è. Entrate.

GORO *(looking in)*: She's home. Come in.

SHARPLESS *(entering alone, knocking quietly)*: Chiedo scusa ... Madama Butterfly ...

SHARPLESS *(entering alone, knocking quietly)*: Excuse me ... Madame Butterfly ...

BUTTERFLY *(her back still turned to the visitor, correcting)*: Madama Pinkerton. Prego. *(Recognizing* SHARPLESS, *happily:)* Oh! *(As* SUZUKI *hastily returns with smoking materials:)* il mio signor Console, signor Console.

BUTTERFLY *(her back still turned to the visitor, correcting)*: Mrs. Pinkerton. Please! *(Recognizing* SHARPLESS, *happily:)* Oh! *(As* SUZUKI *hastily returns with smoking materials:)* Consul, Consul!

SHARPLESS *(surprised)*: Mi ravvisate?

SHARPLESS *(surprised)*: You recognize me?

BUTTERFLY: Benvenuto in casa americana.

BUTTERFLY: Welcome to an American home.

SHARPLESS: Grazie.

SHARPLESS: Thank you.

Invited to sit down, SHARPLESS *drops onto a cushion in discomfort as* BUTTERFLY *smiles behind her fan.*

BUTTERFLY *(graciously)*: Avi, antenati tutti bene?

BUTTERFLY *(graciously)*: Are your ancestors and forebears all well?

SHARPLESS *(smiling in thanks)*: Ma spero.

BUTTERFLY *(signaling to* SUZUKI *to prepare the pipe)*: Fumate?

SHARPLESS: Grazie. *(Taking a letter from his pocket, purposefully:)* Ho qui ...

BUTTERFLY: Signore, io vedo il cielo azzurro. *(Puffs at the pipe, offers it to him.)*

SHARPLESS *(refusing)*: Grazie. ... *(Resuming:)* Ho ...

BUTTERFLY *(putting down the pipe)*: Preferite forse le sigarette americane? *(Offers one.)*

SHARPLESS *(accepting it)*: Grazie. *(Resuming, standing up:)* Ho da mostrarvi ...

BUTTERFLY *(with a lighted match)*: A voi.

SHARPLESS *(smiling in thanks)*: Well, I hope so.

BUTTERFLY *(signaling to* SUZUKI *to prepare the pipe)*: Do you smoke?

SHARPLESS: Thanks. *(Taking a letter from his pocket, purposefully:)* I have here ...

BUTTERFLY: Sir, the skies are blue for me. *(Puffs at the pipe, offers it to him.)*

SHARPLESS *(refusing)*: No, thanks ... *(Resuming:)* I have ...

BUTTERFLY *(putting down the pipe)*: Maybe you prefer American cigarettes? *(Offers one.)*

SHARPLESS *(accepting it)*: Thanks. *(Resuming, standing up:)* I have something to show you ...

BUTTERFLY *(with a lighted match)*: For you.

SHARPLESS *lights the cigarette, puts it down, shows the letter, sits on stool.*

SHARPLESS: Mi scrisse Benjamin Franklin Pinkerton.

BUTTERFLY *(most eagerly)*: Davvero! È in salute?

SHARPLESS: Perfetta.

BUTTERFLY *(getting up, joyfully)*: Io son la donna più lieta del Giappone. Potrei farvi una domanda?

SHARPLESS: Benjamin Franklin Pinkerton has written to me.

BUTTERFLY *(most eagerly)*: Really? Is he well?

SHARPLESS: Perfectly.

BUTTERFLY *(getting up, joyfully)*: I'm the happiest woman in Japan. May I ask you a question?

SHARPLESS: Certo.

BUTTERFLY *(sitting down)*: Quando fanno il lor nido in America i pettirossi?

SHARPLESS *(thunderstruck)*: Come dite?

BUTTERFLY: Sì, ... prima o dopo di qui?

SHARPLESS: Ma perchè?

SHARPLESS: Of course.

BUTTERFLY *(sitting down)*: When do the robins make their nest in America?

SHARPLESS *(thunderstruck)*: What did you say?

BUTTERFLY: Yes ... before or after they do here?

SHARPLESS: But why?

GORO *now listens at the entrance to the terrace.* SUZUKI *is preparing tea.*

BUTTERFLY: Mio marito m'ha promesso di ritornar nella stagion beata che il pettirosso rifà la nidiata. Qui l'ha rifatta per ben tre volte ma può darsi che di là usi nidiar men spesso. *(As* GORO *bursts out laughing:)* Chi ride? Oh, c'è il nakodo! *(Quietly to* SHARPLESS:*)* Un uom cattivo.

GORO *(bowing obsequiously)*: Godo ...

BUTTERFLY *(to* GORO*)*: Zitto. *(*GORO *leaves. To* SHARPLESS:*)* Egli osò ... No ... prima rispondete alla dimanda mia.

SHARPLESS *(embarrassed)*: Mi rincresce, ma ignoro ... Non ho studiato ornitologia.

BUTTERFLY: Orni ...

BUTTERFLY: My husband promised me he would return in the blessed season when the robin makes its nest again. Here it has remade it a good three times but maybe over there it's accustomed to nest less often. *(As* GORO *bursts out laughing:)* Who's laughing? Oh, it's the *nakōdo* [marriage broker]! *(Quietly to* SHARPLESS:*)* A bad man.

GORO *(bowing obsequiously)*: My pleasure ...

BUTTERFLY *(to* GORO*)*: Silence! *(*GORO *leaves. To* SHARPLESS:*)* He had the nerve ... No ... first answer my question.

SHARPLESS *(embarrassed)*: I'm sorry, I don't know ... I haven't studied ornithology.

BUTTERFLY: Orni—?

SHARPLESS: —tologia.

BUTTERFLY: Non lo sapete insomma.

SHARPLESS: No. *(Resuming his errand:)* Dicevamo ...

BUTTERFLY *(her mind on other things)*: Ah, sì. Goro, appena B. F. Pinkerton fu in mare mi venne ad assediare con ciarle e con presenti per ridarmi ora questo, or quel marito. Or promette tesori per uno scimunito ...

GORO *(entering, in self-justification)*: Il ricco Yamadori. Ella è povera in canna. I suoi parenti l'han tutti rinnegata.

SHARPLESS: —thology.

BUTTERFLY: What it comes down to is, you don't know.

SHARPLESS: No. *(Resuming his errand:)* We were saying ...

BUTTERFLY *(her mind on other things)*: Oh, yes. Goro, as soon as B. F. Pinkerton was back at sea, started besieging me with prattle and gifts in order to bestow new husbands on me, now this one, now that one. At the moment he is promising me treasures on behalf of a nitwit ...

GORO *(entering, in self-justification)*: The rich Yamadori. She's as poor as a churchmouse. All her relatives have disowned her.

YAMADORI *is seen in the garden with his servants.*[24]

BUTTERFLY *(seeing him, with a smile)*: Eccolo, attenti!

BUTTERFLY *(seeing him, with a smile)*: Here he is. Watch!

YAMADORI *takes a seat on the terrace.* BUTTERFLY *kneels to him.*

BUTTERFLY: Yamadori — ancor le pene dell'amor non v'han deluso? Vi tagliate ancor le vene se il mio bacio vi ricuso?

YAMADORI: Tra le cose più moleste è l'inutil sospirar.

BUTTERFLY: Yamadori, haven't the sorrows of love disappointed you yet? Are you still going to cut your veins if I refuse you my kiss?

YAMADORI: One of the most unpleasant things is to sigh in vain.

BUTTERFLY *(mocking him gracefully)*: Tante mogli omai togliste, vi doveste abituar.

YAMADORI: L'ho sposate tutte quante e il divorzio mi francò.

BUTTERFLY: Obbligata.

{ YAMADORI: A voi però giurerei fede costante.

SHARPLESS *(putting the letter away, to himself)*: (Il messaggio, ho gran paura, a trasmetter non riesco.)

GORO *(to* SHARPLESS *with emphasis, indicating* YAMADORI*)*: Ville, servi, oro, ad Omara un palazzo principesco.

BUTTERFLY *(seriously)*: Già legata è la mia fede ...

GORO AND YAMADORI *(to* SHARPLESS*)*: Maritata ancor si crede.

BUTTERFLY *(rising)*: Non mi credo, sono, sono!

GORO: Ma la legge ...

BUTTERFLY: Io non la so.

GORO: ... per la moglie, l'abbandono al divorzio equiparò.

BUTTERFLY: La legge giapponese ... non già del mio paese.

GORO: Quale?

BUTTERFLY *(mocking him gracefully)*: You have taken so many wives by now, you should have grown used to it.

YAMADORI: I married them all, and was set free by divorce.

BUTTERFLY: Much obliged!

{ YAMADORI: But to you I would swear eternal constancy.

SHARPLESS *(putting the letter away, to himself)*: (I very much fear I won't manage to deliver the message.)

GORO *(to* SHARPLESS *with emphasis, indicating* YAMADORI*)*: Villas, servants, gold, a princely palace at Omara.

BUTTERFLY *(seriously)*: My faith has already been plighted ...

GORO AND YAMADORI *(to* SHARPLESS*)*: She thinks she's still married.

BUTTERFLY *(rising)*: I don't *think* so—I am, I am!

GORO: But the law ...

BUTTERFLY: I don't know it.

GORO: ... has stipulated that, for the wife, desertion is tantamount to divorce.

BUTTERFLY: Japanese law ... but not the law of my country.

GORO: Which is that?

BUTTERFLY: Gli Stati Uniti ...

SHARPLESS *(to himself)*: (Oh, l'infelice!)

BUTTERFLY *(becoming heated)*: Si sa che aprir la porta e la moglie cacciar per la più corta qui divorziar si dice. Ma in America questo non si può. *(To* SHARPLESS:*)* Vero?

SHARPLESS *(embarrassed)*: Vero ... Però ...

BUTTERFLY *(to the others, triumphantly)*: Là un bravo giudice serio, impettito dice al marito: "Lei vuol andarsene? Sentiam perchè?" "Sono seccato del coniugato!" E il magistraro: "Ah, mascalzone, presto in prigione!" *(Abruptly:)* Suzuki, il thè.

BUTTERFLY: The United States ...

SHARPLESS *(to himself)*: (Oh, the poor woman!)

BUTTERFLY *(becoming heated)*: Everyone knows that, here, opening your door and driving out your wife in the quickest way, is called getting a divorce. But in America that's impossible. *(To* SHARPLESS:*)* Right?

SHARPLESS *(embarrassed)*: Right ... But ...

BUTTERFLY *(to the others, triumphantly)*: There a worthy judge, serious, self-important, says to the husband: "You want to pick up and leave? Tell me why." "I'm fed up with married life!" And the magistrate: "Oh, you scoundrel, march right into jail!" *(Abruptly:)* Suzuki, the tea!

While she goes to pour the tea into cups, the men speak very quietly.

YAMADORI *(to* SHARPLESS*)*: Udiste?

SHARPLESS: Mi rattrista una sì piena cecità.

GORO: Segnalata è già la nave di Pinkerton.

YAMADORI *(in despair)*: Quand'essa lo riveda ...

YAMADORI *(to* SHARPLESS*)*: Did you hear?

SHARPLESS: Such complete blindness makes me sad.

GORO: Pinkerton's ship has already been reported.

YAMADORI *(in despair)*: When she sees him again ...

SHARPLESS: Egli non vuol mostrarsi. Io venni appunto per levarla d'inganno ...

BUTTERFLY *(returning with the tea, to* SHARPLESS*)*: Vostra Grazia permette? *(Laughing behind her fan, with reference to the two others:)* Che persone moleste!

YAMADORI *(refusing tea, rising to go, sighing)*: Addio. Vi lascio il cuor pien di cordoglio: ma spero ancor ...

BUTTERFLY: Padrone.

YAMADORI *(turning back once more)*: Ah! ... se voleste ...

BUTTERFLY: Il guaio è che non voglio ...

SHARPLESS: He doesn't want to show himself here. I came on purpose to tell her she's been deluding herself ...

BUTTERFLY *(returning with the tea, to* SHARPLESS*)*: May I, Your Honor? *(Laughing behind her fan, with reference to the two others:)* What bothersome people!

YAMADORI *(refusing tea, rising to go, sighing)*: Goodbye. I leave behind my heart full of suffering. But I still have hopes ...

BUTTERFLY: Suit yourself.

YAMADORI *(turning back once more)*: Ah, if you only wanted ...

BUTTERFLY: The problem is: I don't want ...

YAMADORI, *his servants and* GORO *leave.* SHARPLESS, *his manner grave, motions* BUTTERFLY *to be seated and takes out the letter.*

SHARPLESS: Ora a noi. Sedete qui; legger con me volete questa lettera?

BUTTERFLY: Date. *(With suitable action:)* Sulla bocca, sul cuore ... *(To* SHARPLESS, *graciously, returning the letter:)* Siete l'uomo migliore del mondo. Incominciate.

SHARPLESS: Now, for the two of us. Sit down here. Do you want to read this letter with me?

BUTTERFLY: Give it to me. *(With suitable action:)* On my lips, on my heart ... *(To* SHARPLESS, *graciously, returning the letter:)* You are the best man in the world. Begin.

SHARPLESS *(reading)*: "Amico, cercherete quel bel fior di fanciulla" ...

BUTTERFLY *(joyfully)*: Dice proprio così?

SHARPLESS: Sì, così dice, ma se ad ogni momento ...

BUTTERFLY *(becoming calm)*: Taccio, taccio, più nulla.

SHARPLESS: "Da quel tempo felice, tre anni son passati."

BUTTERFLY *(interrupting)*: Anche lui li ha contati!

SHARPLESS: "E forse Butterfly non mi rammenta più."

BUTTERFLY *(surprised)*: Non lo rammento? Suzuki, dillo tu. "Non mi rammenta più!"

SHARPLESS *(reading)*: "My friend, please look up that lovely flower of a girl" ...

BUTTERFLY *(joyfully)*: Are those his very words?

SHARPLESS: Yes, they are, but if you interrupt every minute ...

BUTTERFLY *(becoming calm)*: I'll be quiet, I'll be quiet, not another word.

SHARPLESS: "Since those happy days, three years have gone by."

BUTTERFLY *(interrupting)*: He counted them, too!

SHARPLESS: "And perhaps Butterfly no longer remembers me."

BUTTERFLY *(surprised)*: I don't remember him? Suzuki, you tell him. "No longer remembers me!"

SUZUKI *exits left with the tea things.*

SHARPLESS *(to himself)*: (Pazienza!) *(Reading:)* "Se mi vuol bene ancor, se m'aspetta" ...

BUTTERFLY: Oh, le dolci parole! *(Taking the letter and kissing it:)* Tu, benedetta!

SHARPLESS *(to himself)*: (Give me strength!) *(Reading:)* "If she still loves me, if she is waiting for me" ...

BUTTERFLY: Oh, those sweet words! *(Taking the letter and kissing it:)* You blessed letter!

SHARPLESS (*reading again, but with emotion in his voice*): "A voi mi raccomando, perchè vogliate con circospezione prepararla" ...

BUTTERFLY: Ritorna ...

SHARPLESS: "— al colpo" ...

BUTTERFLY (*jumping for joy and clapping her hands*): Quando? presto! presto!

SHARPLESS (*giving up, rising, putting away the letter, to himself*): (Benone. Qui troncarla conviene ... Quel diavolo d'un Pinkerton!) (*Very gravely:*) Ebbene, che fareste, Madama Butterfly, s'ei non dovesse ritornar più mai?

SHARPLESS (*reading again, but with emotion in his voice*): "I beg you to be good enough to use discretion and prepare her" ...

BUTTERFLY: He's coming back ...

SHARPLESS: "—for the blow" ...

BUTTERFLY (*jumping for joy and clapping her hands*): When? Quick! Quick!

SHARPLESS (*giving up, rising, putting away the letter, to himself*): (All right now! This is the moment to cut it short ... That devil Pinkerton!) (*Very gravely:*) Very well, then, what would you do, Madame Butterfly, if he were never to return again?

BUTTERFLY *stands motionless as if she had received a death blow, bows her head, then speaks with childlike submissiveness.*

BUTTERFLY: Due cose potrei far: tornar ... a divertir la gente col cantar ... oppur, ... meglio, morire.

BUTTERFLY: I could do two things: go back ... to entertaining people with my singing ... or else ... preferably—die.

SHARPLESS *walks up and down in agitation, then takes her hands and speaks paternally.*

SHARPLESS: Di strapparvi assai mi costa dai miraggi ingannatori. Accogliete la proposta di quel ricco Yamadori.

SHARPLESS: It's very hard on me to tear you away from your deceptive illusions. Accept the proposal of that rich Yamadori.

BUTTERFLY *(pulling away her hands)*: Voi, voi, signor, ... mi dite questo! ... Voi?

SHARPLESS *(embarrassed)*: Santo Dio, come si fa?

BUTTERFLY *(clapping for* SUZUKI*)*: Qui, Suzuki, presto, presto, che Sua Grazia se ne va.

SHARPLESS: Mi scacciate?

BUTTERFLY *(bringing him back repentantly)*: Ve ne prego: già l'insistere non vale. *(Motions* SUZUKI *into the garden.)*

SHARPLESS *(apologetically)*: Fui brutale, non lo nego.

BUTTERFLY *(hand on heart)*: Oh, mi fate tanto male, tanto male, tanto, tanto! *(Tottering, then getting hold of herself:)* Niente, ... niente! ... Ho creduto morir ... Ma passa presto come passan le nuvole sul mare ... Ah! m'ha scordata?

BUTTERFLY *(pulling away her hands)*: You, you, sir, say that to me?! ... You?

SHARPLESS *(embarrassed)*: Merciful heaven, what am I to do?

BUTTERFLY *(clapping for* SUZUKI*)*: Here, Suzuki, quickly, quickly, because His Honor is going.

SHARPLESS: You're throwing me out?

BUTTERFLY *(bringing him back repentantly)*: Please: it will do no good to harp on it. *(Motions* SUZUKI *into the garden.)*

SHARPLESS *(apologetically)*: I was brutal, I don't deny it.

BUTTERFLY *(hand on heart)*: Oh, you have hurt me so much, hurt me so much, so much, so much! *(Tottering, then getting hold of herself:)* It's nothing ... nothing! ... I thought I was dying ... But it passes quickly, the way clouds pass over the sea ... Ah! Has he forgotten me?

Running into the room at left, she proudly brings back her baby on her shoulder.

BUTTERFLY: E questo? ... E questo? ... E questo egli potrà pure scordare? ... *(She puts down the baby, but holds him close.)*

BUTTERFLY: And him? ... And him? ... And will he be able to forget him, too? ... *(She puts down the baby, but holds him close.)*

SHARPLESS *(with emotion)*: Egli è suo?

BUTTERFLY: Chi vide mai a bimbo del Giappon occhi azzurrini? E il labbro? E i ricciolini d'oro schietto?

SHARPLESS: È palese, e Pinkerton lo sa?

BUTTERFLY: No. No. È nato quand'egli stava in quel suo gran paese. *(Caressing the baby:)* Ma voi ... gli scriverete che l'aspetta un figlio senza pari! E mi saprete dir s'ei non s'affretta per le terre e pei mari! *(Seats the baby on a cushion, kneels by him and kisses him.)* Sai cos'ebbe cuore di pensare quel signore *(indicating* SHARPLESS*)*? Che tua madre dovrà prenderti in braccio ed alla pioggia e al vento andar per la città a guadagnarti[25] il pane e il vestimento. Ed alle impietosite genti ... la man tremante stenderà gridando: ... Udite, udite la triste mia canzon. A un'infelice madre la carità, muovetevi a pietà ... *(Rising:)* E Butterfly, orribile destino, danzerà per te ... E come fece già la ghescia canterà! E la canzon giuliva e lieta in un singhiozzo finirà! Ah! no, no! questo mai! questo mestier che al disonore porta! Morta! morta! Mai più danzar! Piuttosto la mia vita vo' troncar!

SHARPLESS *(with emotion)*: Is he his child?

BUTTERFLY: Who ever saw a Japanese child with blue eyes? And his mouth? And the curls of pure gold?

SHARPLESS: It's obvious. And does Pinkerton know?

BUTTERFLY: No. No. He was born while he was in that big country of his. *(Caressing the baby:)* But you ... will write and tell him that a matchless son is waiting for him! And then you'll see if he doesn't hurry back over land and sea! *(Seats the baby on a cushion, kneels by him and kisses him.)* Do you know what that gentleman *(indicating* SHARPLESS*)* had the heart to think? That your mother will have to take you in her arms and go through the city in the rain and wind to earn your bread and clothing. And she will stretch out her trembling hand to the people who have been moved to pity, crying: "Listen, listen to my sad song. Charity for an unhappy mother, have pity" ... *(Rising:)* And Butterfly— horrible fate—will dance for your sake ... And as she used to do, the geisha will sing! And the jolly, happy song will end in a sob! Oh, no, no! That— never! That profession which

Ah! ... Morta! *(She drops to the floor, hugging the baby.)*

SHARPLESS *(to himself, weeping)*: (Quanta pietà) *(To her, more calmly:)* Io scendo al piano. Mi perdonate? ...

BUTTERFLY *(rising, shaking his hand, says to the baby)*: A te, dàgli la mano.

SHARPLESS: I bei capelli biondi! *(Kisses the baby.)* Caro, come ti chiamano?

BUTTERFLY *(to the baby)*: Rispondi: Oggi il mio nome è Dolore. *(To* SHARPLESS:*)* Però dite al babbo, scrivendogli, che il giorno del suo ritorno, Gioia, Gioia ... mi chiamerò! [26]

SHARPLESS: Tuo padre lo saprà, te lo prometto ... *(Bows, leaves.)*

SUZUKI *(offstage)*: Vespa! Rospo maledetto!

leads to dishonor! I'll die! Die! But never dance again! I will sooner put an end to my life! Ah, ... I'll die! *(She drops to the floor, hugging the baby.)*

SHARPLESS *(to himself, weeping)*: (How pitiful!) *(To her, more calmly:)* I'm going down to the lower city. Can you forgive me? ...

BUTTERFLY *(rising, shaking his hand, says to the baby)*: You, give him your hand.

SHARPLESS: That beautiful blonde hair! *(Kisses the baby.)* What's your name, little one?

BUTTERFLY *(to the baby)*: Answer: "Today my name is Trouble." *(To* SHARPLESS:*)* But tell his father, in a letter: "On the day he returns, I will be called Joy, Joy!"

SHARPLESS: Your father will be told, I promise you ... *(Bows, leaves.)*

SUZUKI *(offstage)*: Insect! Damned toad!

She enters, dragging in the reluctant GORO, *who cries out.*

BUTTERFLY: Che fu?

SUZUKI: Ci ronza intorno il vampiro! e ogni giorno ai quattro venti spargendo va che niuno sa chi padre al bimbo sia! *(She releases him.)*

BUTTERFLY: What happened?

SUZUKI: This vampire loiters around the place, and every day he spreads the word to all and sundry that no one knows who the baby's father is! *(She releases him.)*

GORO: Dicevo ... solo ... che là in America quando un figliolo è nato maledetto trarrà sempre reietto la vita fra le genti!

BUTTERFLY *(shrieking, taking her father's suicide knife from its shrine)*: Ah! tu menti! menti! menti! Ah! menti! *(Seizing the wailing* GORO:*)* Dillo ancora e t'uccido! ...

SUZUKI *(taking the baby into the room at the left)*: No!

BUTTERFLY *(spurning* GORO *with her foot)*: Va via!

GORO: I ... only ... said that there in America when a child is born unlawfully he always spends his life as an outcast from society!

BUTTERFLY *(shrieking, taking her father's suicide knife from its shrine)*: Ah, you're lying! You're lying! You're lying! Ah, you're lying! *(Seizing the wailing* GORO:*)* Say that again and I'll kill you! ...

SUZUKI *(taking the baby into the room at the left)*: Don't!

BUTTERFLY *(spurning* GORO *with her foot)*: Get out!

He flees. She rouses herself and puts away the knife.

BUTTERFLY: Vedrai, piccolo amor, mia pena e mio conforto, mio piccolo amor ... Ah! vedrai che il tuo vendicator ... ci porterà lontano, lontan, nella sua terra, lontan ci porterà ...

BUTTERFLY: You'll see, my little darling, my sorrow and my consolation, my little darling ... Oh, you'll see how your avenger ... will take us far, far away, to his country, will take us far away ...

A cannon shot is heard.

SUZUKI *(entering breathlessly)*: Il cannone del porto! *(Running to the terrace with* BUTTERFLY:*)* Una nave da guerra ...

BUTTERFLY: Bianca ... bianca ... il vessillo americano delle

SUZUKI *(entering breathlessly)*: The harbor cannon! *(Running to the terrace with* BUTTERFLY:*)* A warship ...

BUTTERFLY: White ... white ... the American flag with its stars

stelle ... Or governa per anco-
rare. *(Getting a telescope and returning to the terrace, trembling
with excitement:)* Reggimi la
mano ch'io ne discerna il
nome, il nome, il nome.
Eccolo: **ABRAMO LIN-
COLN!** *(Giving the telescope to
suzuki and reentering the room:)*
Tutti han mentito! tutti ...
tutti! ... sol io lo sapevo ... sol
io che l'amo. Vedi lo scimunito
tuo dubbio? È giunto! è
giunto! è giunto! proprio nel
punto che ognun diceva:
piangi e dispera ... Trionfa il
mio amor! il mio amor, la mia
fe' trionfa intera: ei torna e
m'ama! *(Runs onto the terrace ju-
bilantly,* suzuki *following.)*
Scuoti quella fronda di ciliegio
e m'innonda di fior ... Io vo'
tuffar nella pioggia odorosa
l'arsa fronte. *(Sobs with tenderness.)*

suzuki *(calming her)*: Signora,
quetatevi ... quel pianto ...

butterfly: No, ... rido, rido!
Quanto lo dovremo aspettar?
... Che pensi? Un'ora?

suzuki: Di più! ...

... Now it's steering into posi-
tion to drop anchor. *(Getting a
telescope and returning to the terrace, trembling with excitement:)*
Steady my hand so I can make
out the name, the name, the
name. There it is: the *Abraham
Lincoln!* *(Giving the telescope to
suzuki and reentering the room:)*
Everybody was lying! Everybody ... everybody! ... I was
the only one who knew ... only
I, who love him. Do you see
how stupid your doubts were?
He has come! He has come!
He has come!—at the very
moment when everyone was
saying: "Weep and despair"
... My love triumphs, my love,
my unbroken faith triumphs:
he is returning and he loves
me! *(Runs onto the terrace jubi-
lantly,* suzuki *following.)* Shake
that cherry branch and cover
me with flowers ... I want to
plunge my fevered brow into
that fragrant downpour. *(Sobs
with tenderness.)*

suzuki *(calming her)*: Mistress,
calm yourself ... that crying
...

butterfly: No, ... I'm laughing, I'm laughing! How long
will we have to wait for him?
... What do you think? An
hour?

suzuki: More! ...

BUTTERFLY: Due ore forse. Tutto ... tutto sia pien di fior, come la notte è di faville.[27] *(Signals to* SUZUKI *to go into the garden.)* Va pei fior ...

SUZUKI *(from the terrace)*: Tutti i fior?

BUTTERFLY: Tutti i fior, tutti ... tutti. Pesco, viola, gelsomin, quanto di cespo, o d'erba, o d'albero fiorì.

SUZUKI: Uno squallor d'inverno sarà tutto il giardin. *(Enters the garden.)*

BUTTERFLY: Tutta la primavera voglio che olezzi qui.

SUZUKI: Uno squallor d'inverno sarà tutto il giardin. *(Appearing below the terrace with a bunch of flowers:)* A voi, signora.

BUTTERFLY *(taking them)*: Cogline ancora. *(Puts flowers in vases.)*

SUZUKI *(back in the garden)*: Soventi a questa siepe veniste a riguardare lungi, piangendo nella deserta immensità.

BUTTERFLY: Giunse l'atteso, nulla più chiedo al mare; diedi pianto alla zolla, essa i suoi fior mi dà.

BUTTERFLY: Two hours maybe. Let everything ... everything be full of flowers as the night is full of stars. *(Signals to* SUZUKI *to go into the garden.)* Go bring the flowers ...

SUZUKI *(from the terrace)*: All the flowers?

BUTTERFLY: All the flowers, all ... all. Peach blossoms, violets, jasmines, every flower that has appeared on a bush, stalk or tree.

SUZUKI: The whole garden will be stripped bare as if in winter! *(Enters the garden.)*

BUTTERFLY: I want all of springtime to shed its fragrance here.

SUZUKI: The whole garden will be stripped bare as if in winter. *(Appearing below the terrace with a bunch of flowers:)* Here, mistress.

BUTTERFLY *(taking them)*: Pick more. *(Puts flowers in vases.)*

SUZUKI *(back in the garden)*: You used to come to this hedge often to look far out, weeping, over the barren expanse of the ocean.

BUTTERFLY: The man I waited for has come; I ask nothing more of the sea. I gave my tears to the soil and it gives me its flowers in return.

SUZUKI *(bringing more flowers)*: Spoglio è l'orto.

BUTTERFLY: Spoglio è l'orto? Vien, m'aiuta.

SUZUKI *(as both of them strew flowers)*: Rose al varco della soglia.

BUTTERFLY AND SUZUKI: Tutta la primavera voglio che olezzi qui.

{ BUTTERFLY: Seminiamo intorno april, seminiamo april! Tutta la primavera voglio che olezzi qui ...

SUZUKI: Seminiamo april. Tutta la primavera, tutta, tutta.

SUZUKI: Gigli? ... viole?

BUTTERFLY: —intorno, intorno spandi.

SUZUKI: Seminiamo intorno april.

BUTTERFLY: Seminiamo intorno april.

{ BUTTERFLY: Il suo sedil s'inghirlandi, di convolvi s'inghirlandi; gigli e viole intorno spandi, —

SUZUKI: Gigli, rose spandi, tutta la primavera, spandi gigli, viole, —

BUTTERFLY AND SUZUKI: — seminiamo intorno april! *(With dancing movements:)* Gettiamo a

SUZUKI *(bringing more flowers)*: The garden is bare.

BUTTERFLY: The garden is bare? Come help me.

SUZUKI *(as both of them strew flowers)*: Roses at the crossing of the threshold.

BUTTERFLY AND SUZUKI: I want all of springtime to shed its fragrance here.

{ BUTTERFLY: Let us sow April all around, let us sow April! I want all of springtime to shed its fragrance here ...

SUZUKI: Let us sow April. All of springtime, all, all.

SUZUKI: Lilies? ... Violets?

BUTTERFLY: Scatter them around, all around.

SUZUKI: Let us sow April all around.

BUTTERFLY: Let us sow April all around.

{ BUTTERFLY: Let his chair be garlanded, garlanded with morning glories; scatter lilies and violets around, —

SUZUKI: Scatter lilies, roses, all of springtime, scatter lilies, violets, —

BUTTERFLY AND SUZUKI: Let us sow April all around! *(With dancing movements:)* Let us toss

mani piene mammole e tube-
rose, corolle di verbene, petali
d'ogni fior! Corolle di verbene,
petali d'ogni fior!

BUTTERFLY *(as the two of them
bring materials for her toilette)*:
Or vienmi ad adornar. *(Sunset
begins.)* No! pria portami il
bimbo. *(*SUZUKI *does so. Looking
into a hand-mirror:)* Non son più
quella! ... Troppi sospiri la
bocca mandò, e l'occhio ri-
guardò nel lontan troppo fiso.[28]
Dammi sul viso un tocco di
carmino ... *(Brushing the baby's
cheeks:)* ed anche a te, piccino,
perche la veglia non ti faccia
vôte per pallore le gote.

SUZUKI: Non vi movete, che v'ho
a ravviare i capelli.

BUTTERFLY: Che ne diranno![29]
... E lo zio Bonzo? ... già del
mio danno tutti contenti! ... E
Yamadori coi suoi languori! ...
Beffati, scornati, beffati, spen-
nati gli ingrati!

SUZUKI: È fatto.

BUTTERFLY: L'obi che vestii da
sposa.[30] Quà, ch'io lo vesta.

handfuls of sweet violets and
tuberoses, corollas of verbena,
petals of every flower! Corollas
of verbena, petals of every
flower!

BUTTERFLY *(as the two of them
bring materials for her toilette)*:
Now come and dress me pro-
perly. *(Sunset begins.)* No! First
bring me the baby. *(*SUZUKI
*does so. Looking into a hand-
mirror:)* I've changed so much!
... My lips have uttered too
many sighs, and my eyes have
stared too hard into the distance. Put a touch of rouge on
my face ... *(Brushing the baby's
cheeks:)* and a touch for you,
too, little one, so that our vigil
doesn't make your cheeks look
hollow with pallor.

SUZUKI: Don't move around, I
have to do your hair.

BUTTERFLY: What will they all
say? ... And my uncle the
bonze? ... They were all so
pleased at my loss! ... And Yamadori with his languishing! ...
They're ridiculous now, put
to shame, ridiculous, left high
and dry—the whole ungrateful
bunch!

SUZUKI: I've finished.

BUTTERFLY: The robe I wore as
a bride. Bring it for me to put
on.

As she dresses, SUZUKI *wraps up the baby in another robe.*

BUTTERFLY: Vo' che mi veda indosso il vel del primo dì. E un papavero rosso nei capelli. Così. *(Motioning* SUZUKI *to close the partition:)* Nella shosi or farem tre forellini per riguardar, e starem zitti come topolini ad aspettar.

BUTTERFLY: I want him to see me wearing what I had on that first night. And a red poppy in my hair. Like this. *(Motioning* SUZUKI *to close the partition:)* Now we'll make three little holes in the *shoji* so we can look out, and we'll be quiet as mice waiting for him.

Night has fallen. BUTTERFLY *leads the baby to the partition and makes three peepholes. Moonbeams illuminate the partition from outside. Eventually the baby and* SUZUKI *fall asleep, but* BUTTERFLY *is completely alert.*

CHORUS *hums from offstage.*

CHORUS *hums from offstage.*

ACT THREE

ACT THREE

The orchestral prelude depicts the passing of the night and the arrival of the morning. The curtain rises on the same scene and same group of figures as at the end of Act Two, but the sun is now out. Sailors' calls are heard from the distant bay.

SAILORS: Oh eh! Oh eh! Oh eh! Oh eh! Oh eh! Oh eh! Oh eh! Oh eh! Oh eh! Oh eh! Oh eh! Oh eh! Oh eh! Oh eh!

SUZUKI *(waking)*: Già il sole! ... *(Touching* BUTTERFLY'S *shoulder:)* Cio-cio-san ...

BUTTERFLY *(rising, says trustingly)*: Verrà ... verrà, vedrai.[31] *(Picks up the sleeping baby.)*

SUZUKI: Salite a riposare, affranta siete ... al suo venire ... vi chiamerò.

BUTTERFLY *(going up the little staircase at left to the upper room)*: Dormi amor mio, dormi sul mio cor. Tu sei con Dio ed io col mio dolor ... A te i rai ... degli astri d'or. Bimbo mio dormi!

SUZUKI: Povera Butterfly! ...

SAILORS: Oh, ho! Oh, ho! Oh, ho! Oh, ho! Oh, ho! Oh, ho! Oh, ho! Oh, ho! Oh, ho! Oh, ho! Oh, ho! Oh, ho! Oh, ho! Oh, ho!

SUZUKI *(waking)*: The sun already! ... *(Touching* BUTTERFLY'S *shoulder:)* Cho-Cho-San ...

BUTTERFLY *(rising, says trustingly)*: He'll come ... he'll come, you'll see. *(Picks up the sleeping baby.)*

SUZUKI: Go up and get some rest, you're all in ... When he comes ... I'll call you.

BUTTERFLY *(going up the little staircase at left to the upper room)*: Sleep, my darling, sleep on my heart. You are with God and I with my trouble ... For you the beams ... of the golden stars. Sleep, my baby!

SUZUKI: Poor Butterfly! ...

BUTTERFLY (*from within*): Dormi amor mio, dormi sul mio cor. Tu sei con Dio ed io col mio dolor ...

SUZUKI: Povera Butterfly! ... (*At a light knock at the door:*) Chi sia? ... (*At a louder knock, she opens.*) Oh!

SHARPLESS (*entering cautiously with* PINKERTON): Stz!

PINKERTON: Zitta! Zitta!

SHARPLESS: Zitta! Zitta!

PINKERTON: Non la destar.

SUZUKI: Era stanca sì tanto! Vi stette ad aspettare tutta la notte col bimbo.

PINKERTON: Come sapea? ...

SUZUKI: Non giunge da tre anni una nave nel porto, che da lunge Butterfly ... non ne scruti il color, la bandiera.

SHARPLESS (*to* PINKERTON): Ve lo dissi?

SUZUKI: La chiamo ...

PINKERTON: No: non ancor.

SUZUKI: Lo vedete, ier sera, la stanza volle sparger di fiori.

SHARPLESS (*with emotion*): Ve lo dissi? ...

PINKERTON (*upset*): Che pena!

BUTTERFLY (*from within*): Sleep, my darling, sleep on my heart. You are with God and I with my trouble ...

SUZUKI: Poor Butterfly! ... (*At a light knock at the door:*) Who can it be? ... (*At a louder knock, she opens.*) Oh!

SHARPLESS (*entering cautiously with* PINKERTON): Sh!

PINKERTON: Quiet! Quiet!

SHARPLESS: Quiet! Quiet!

PINKERTON: Don't wake her up.

SUZUKI: She was so tired! She was waiting for you all night with the baby.

PINKERTON: How did she know ...?

SUZUKI: For three years not a ship has arrived in the harbor without Butterfly studying its color and flag from up here.

SHARPLESS (*to* PINKERTON): Didn't I tell you?

SUZUKI: I'll call her ...

PINKERTON: No, not yet.

SUZUKI: You see? Last night she insisted on scattering flowers around the room.

SHARPLESS (*with emotion*): Didn't I tell you? ...

PINKERTON (*upset*): How sad!

SUZUKI *(hearing a sound)*: Chi c'è là fuori nel giardino? *(Looking out:)* Una donna!...

PINKERTON *(bringing her downstage again)*: Zitta!

SUZUKI *(in agitation)*: Chi è? chi è?

SHARPLESS: Meglio dirle ogni cosa...

SUZUKI: Chi è? chi è?

PINKERTON *(embarrassed)*: È venuta con me.[32]

SUZUKI: Chi è? chi è?

SHARPLESS *(firmly)*: È sua moglie!

SUZUKI *(hearing a sound)*: Who is out there in the garden? *(Looking out:)* A woman!...

PINKERTON *(bringing her downstage again)*: Quiet!

SUZUKI *(in agitation)*: Who is she? Who is she?

SHARPLESS: It's better to tell her everything...

SUZUKI: Who is she? Who is she?

PINKERTON *(embarrassed)*: She came with me.

SUZUKI: Who is she? Who is she?

SHARPLESS *(firmly)*: She's his wife!

SUZUKI *raises her arms skyward, then falls to her knees with her face to the ground.*

SUZUKI: Anime sante degli avi! Alla piccina s'è spento il sol, ... s'è spento il sol!...

SHARPLESS *(calming her and lifting her up)*: Scegliemmo quest'ora mattutina per ritrovarti sola, Suzuki, e alla gran prova un aiuto, un sostegno cercar con te.

SUZUKI *(despairingly)*: Che giova? ... che giova?...

SUZUKI: Holy spirits of my ancestors! The little girl's sun has stopped shining, ... her sun has stopped shining!...

SHARPLESS *(calming her and lifting her up)*: We chose this early morning hour in order to find you alone, Suzuki, and together with you look for some aid and support in this great ordeal.

SUZUKI *(despairingly)*: What's the good? What's the good?

SHARPLESS *takes* SUZUKI *aside to gain her aid, while* PINKERTON *nervously paces the room, studying its details.*

SHARPLESS: Io so che alle sue pene non ci sono conforti! Ma del bimbo conviene assicurar le sorti!

PINKERTON: Oh, l'amara fragranza di questi fior, ... velenosa al cor mi va. Immutata è la stanza dei nostri amor ... Ma un gel di morte vi sta. *(Seeing a picture of himself:)* Il mio ritratto ... Tre anni son passati, tre anni son passati, tre anni son passati e noverati n'ha i giorni e l'ore, i giorni e l'ore!

SHARPLESS: La pietosa che entrar non osa materna cura del bimbo avrà. Suvvia, parla, suvvia, parla con quella pia e conducila qui ... s'anche la veda Butterfly, non importa. Anzi, meglio se accorta del vero si facesse alla sua vista. Suvvia, parla con quella pia, suvvia, conducila qui, conducila qui ...

SUZUKI: Oh, me trista! E volete ch'io chieda ad una madre ... E volete ch'io chieda ad una madre ... Oh! me trista! Oh! me trista! Anime sante degli avi! ... Alla piccina s'è spento il sol! Oh! me trista! Anime

SHARPLESS: I know that for her sorrows there are no consolations! But we must protect the baby's future.

PINKERTON: Oh, the bitter fragrance of these flowers ... is like poison to my heart. The room in which we loved is unchanged ... But there is a deathly chill in it. *(Seeing a picture of himself:)* My portrait ... Three years have gone by, three years have gone by, three years have gone by and she has counted every day and hour of them, every day and hour!

SHARPLESS: That compassionate woman who is afraid to come inside will take care of the baby like a mother. Come, talk, come, talk to that affectionate woman and bring her here ... Even if Butterfly should see her, it doesn't matter. In fact, it would be better if she were to become aware of the truth by seeing her. Come, talk to that affectionate woman, come, bring her here, bring her here ...

SUZUKI: Oh, wretch that I am! And you want me to ask a mother ... And you want me to ask a mother ... Oh, wretch that I am! Oh, wretch that I am! Holy spirits of my ancestors! ... The little girl's sun has

sante degli avi! ... Alla piccina s'è spento il sol! ...

SHARPLESS *(forcing* SUZUKI *into the garden)*: Vien, Suzuki, vien!

PINKERTON *(to* SHARPLESS, *who approaches him)*: Non posso rimaner, ...

SUZUKI *(going)*: Oh! me trista!

PINKERTON: Sharpless, v'aspetto per via.

SHARPLESS: Non ve l'avevo detto?

PINKERTON: Datele voi qualche soccorso: mi struggo dal rimorso, mi struggo dal rimorso ...

SHARPLESS: Vel dissi? vi ricorda? quando la man vi diede: "badate! Ella ci crede" e fui profeta allor! ... Sorda ai consigli, sorda ai dubbî, vilipesa ... nell'ostinata attesa raccolse il cor.

PINKERTON: Sì, tutto in un istante io vedo il fallo mio ... e sento che di questo tormento tregua mai non avrò, mai non avrò! no!

stopped shining! Oh, wretch that I am! Holy spirits of my ancestors! ... The little girl's sun has stopped shining! ...

SHARPLESS *(forcing* SUZUKI *into the garden)*: Come, Suzuki, come!

PINKERTON *(to* SHARPLESS, *who approaches him)*: I can't stay, ...

SUZUKI *(going)*: Oh, wretch that I am!

PINKERTON: Sharpless, I'll wait for you along the way.

SHARPLESS: Didn't I tell you all this?

PINKERTON: Give her some aid, won't you? I am consumed with remorse, I am consumed with remorse ...

SHARPLESS: I told you— remember?—when she gave you her hand: "Look out! She believes in all this." And I was a prophet then! ... She was deaf to advice, deaf to all doubts, and though she was reviled, her heart was absorbed in her stubborn expectation of your return.

PINKERTON: Yes, all in a flash I see my mistake ... and I feel that this torment will never give me a minute's peace, never! No!

SHARPLESS: Andate: il triste vero da sola apprenderà ...

PINKERTON *(lamenting)*: Addio, fiorito asil di letizia e d'amor ... Sempre il mite suo sembiante con strazio atroce vedrò ...

SHARPLESS: Ma or quel cor sincero presago è già.

PINKERTON: Addio, fiorito asil ...

SHARPLESS: Vel dissi, vi ricorda? e fui profeta allor.

PINKERTON: —non reggo al tuo squallor, ah, non reggo al tuo squallor. Fuggo, fuggo: son vil! Addio, non reggo al tuo squallor, —

{
SHARPLESS: Andate, il triste vero apprenderà.

PINKERTON: —ah! son vil, ah! son vil! ...
}

SHARPLESS: Go. She'll learn the sad truth by herself ...

PINKERTON *(lamenting)*: Farewell, flowery refuge of gladness and love ... I will constantly see her gentle face and will be cruelly tortured ...

SHARPLESS: But now that forthright heart is already full of foreboding.

PINKERTON: Farewell, flowery refuge ...

SHARPLESS: I told you—remember?—and I was a prophet then.

PINKERTON: — I can't stand seeing you despoiled, ah, I can't stand seeing you despoiled. I'm running away, I'm running away: I'm contemptible! Farewell, I can't stand seeing you despoiled, —

{
SHARPLESS: Go; she will learn the sad truth.

PINKERTON: — ah, I'm contemptible, ah, I'm contemptible! ...
}

PINKERTON *wrings* SHARPLESS' *hands and quickly exits right.* KATE *and* SUZUKI *enter from the garden,* KATE *stopping at the foot of the terrace.*

KATE *(gently to* SUZUKI*)*: Glielo dirai?

SUZUKI *(stiffly)*: Prometto.

KATE *(gently to* SUZUKI*)*: Will you tell her?

SUZUKI *(stiffly)*: I promise.

KATE: E le darai consiglio d'affidarmi? ...

SUZUKI: Prometto.

KATE: Lo terrò come un figlio.

SUZUKI: Vi credo. Ma bisogna ch'io le sia sola accanto ... Nella grande ora ... sola! Piangerà tanto tanto! piangerà tanto!

BUTTERFLY *(from the room at left)*: Suzuki! ... Suzuki! ... Dove sei? Suzuki! *(Appears at door.)*

SUZUKI: Son qui ... pregavo e rimettevo a posto ... *(Hastily preventing* BUTTERFLY *from entering:)* No ... no ... no ... no ... no ... non scendete ... *(In a futile effort to restrain her:)* No ... no ... no ...

BUTTERFLY *(pacing the room in joyful excitement)*: È qui ... è qui ... dove è nascosto? è qui ... è qui ... Ecco il Console ... *(Becoming alarmed:)* e dove? ... dove? ... *(After searching everywhere:)* Non c'è! ... *(To* SHARPLESS:*)* Quella donna? Che vuol da me? Niuno parla ... Perche piangete?[33] No: non ditemi nulla ... nulla ... forse potrei cader morta sull'attimo ... Tu, Suzuki, che sei tanto buona, non piangere! e mi vuoi

KATE: And you"ll advise her to let me have him? ...

SUZUKI: I promise.

KATE: I'll treat him like my own son.

SUZUKI: I believe you. But I must be the only one with her ... at the awful moment ... the only one! She'll cry so hard, so hard! She'll cry so hard!

BUTTERFLY *(from the room at left)*: Suzuki! ... Suzuki! ... Where are you? Suzuki! *(Appears at door.)*

SUZUKI: I'm here ... I was praying and putting things in order ... *(Hastily preventing* BUTTERFLY *from entering:)* No ... no ... no ... no ... no ... don't come down ... *(In a futile effort to restrain her:)* No ... no ... no ...

BUTTERFLY *(pacing the room in joyful excitement)*: He's here ... he's here ... where is he hiding? He's here ... he's here ... There's the Consul ... *(Becoming alarmed:)* And where ... ? where ... ? *(After searching everywhere:)* He's not here! *(To* SHARPLESS:*)* That woman? What does she want of me? No one is saying anything ... Why are you crying? No: don't tell me anything ... I might fall down dead on the spot ...

tanto bene, un Sì, un No, di'
piano: Vive?

SUZUKI: Sì.

BUTTERFLY *(stricken)*: Ma non
viene più. Te l'han detto!
(Angered at her silence:) Vespa!
Voglio che tu risponda.

SUZUKI: Mai più.

BUTTERFLY *(coldly)*: Ma è
giunto ieri?

SUZUKI: Sì.

BUTTERFLY *(as if spellbound at the
sight of* KATE*)*: Ah! quella
donna mi fa tanta paura! tanta
paura![34]

SHARPLESS: È la causa innocente
d'ogni vostra sciagura. Perdo-
natele.

BUTTERFLY: Ah! è sua moglie!
(In calm tones:) Tutto è morto
per me! tutto è finito! Ah!

SHARPLESS: Coraggio.

BUTTERFLY: Voglion prendermi
tutto! il figlio mio!

SHARPLESS: Fatelo pel suo bene il
sacrifizio . . .

You, Suzuki, who are so
kind—don't cry!—and who
love me so much, say yes or no,
tell me quietly: Is he alive?

SUZUKI: Yes.

BUTTERFLY *(stricken)*: But he's
not coming any more. They
told you! *(Angered at her silence:)* Insect! I want you to
answer!

SUZUKI: He's never coming.

BUTTERFLY *(coldly)*: But he arrived yesterday?

SUZUKI: Yes.

BUTTERFLY *(as if spellbound at the
sight of* KATE*)*: Ah! That
woman makes me so scared! So
scared!

SHARPLESS: She is the innocent
cause of all your misfortunes.
Forgive her.

BUTTERFLY: Ah! She's his wife!
(In calm tones:) Everything is
dead for me! Everything is
over! Ah!

SHARPLESS: Be brave.

BUTTERFLY: They want to take
everything away from me! My
son!

SHARPLESS: Make the sacrifice
for his good . . .

BUTTERFLY: Ah! triste madre! triste madre! Abbandonar ... mio figlio! E sia! A lui devo obbedir!

KATE *(from outside)*: Potete perdonarmi, Butterfly? ...

BUTTERFLY *(solemnly)*: Sotto il gran ponte del cielo non v'è donna di voi più felice. Siatelo sempre, non v'attristate per me[35] ...

KATE *(to* SHARPLESS*)*: Povera piccina!

SHARPLESS: È un'immensa pietà!

KATE: E il figlio lo darà?

BUTTERFLY *(who has heard)*: A lui lo potrò dare se lo verrà a cercare. *(Meaningfully:)* Fra mezz'ora salite la collina.[36]

BUTTERFLY: Oh, unhappy mother! Unhappy mother! To give up ... my son! Very well! I must obey him!

KATE *(from outside)*: Can you ever forgive me, Butterfly? ...

BUTTERFLY *(solemnly)*: Under the great bridge of heaven there is no woman luckier than you. May you always be so; don't grieve over me ...

KATE *(to* SHARPLESS*)*: Poor little thing!

SHARPLESS: It's a tremendous shame!

KATE: And will she hand over her son?

BUTTERFLY *(who has heard)*: I will be ready to give the child to him if he comes to get him. *(Meaningfully:)* Come back up the hill in half an hour.

SUZUKI *shows out the visitors, then hastens to aid* BUTTERFLY, *who has fallen. She places her hand on her mistress' heart.*

SUZUKI: Come una mosca prigioniera l'ali batte il piccolo cuor!

BUTTERFLY *(recovering and pulling away)*: Troppa luce è di fuor, e troppa primavera. Chiudi. *(When the room is dark:)* Il bimbo ove sia?

SUZUKI: Your little heart is fluttering its wings like a trapped fly!

BUTTERFLY *(recovering and pulling away)*: There's too much light outside, and too much springtime. Close things up. *(When the room is dark:)* Where is the baby?

SUZUKI: Giuoca ... Lo chiamo?

BUTTERFLY *(anguished)*: Lascialo giuocar, lascialo giuocar. Va a fargli compagnia.[37]

SUZUKI *(in tears)*: Resto con voi.

BUTTERFLY *(clapping loudly)*: Va, va. Te lo comando.

SUZUKI: Playing ... Should I call him?

BUTTERFLY *(anguished)*: Let him play, let him play. Go keep him company.

SUZUKI *(in tears)*: I'm staying with you.

BUTTERFLY *(clapping loudly)*: Go, go! I order you!

SUZUKI *goes.* BUTTERFLY *kneels in front of the Buddha and remains in silence for a while, then unveils the knife, piously kisses the blade and reads aloud the words inscribed on it.*

BUTTERFLY: "Con onor muore chi non può serbar vita con onore."

BUTTERFLY: "Death with honor for those who cannot live with honor."

As she points the knife at her throat, SUZUKI'S *arm is seen pushing in the baby at the door, left.* BUTTERFLY *drops the knife and hugs the baby passionately.*

BUTTERFLY: Tu? tu? tu? tu? tu? tu? tu? piccolo Iddio! Amore, amore mio, fior di giglio e di rosa. Non saperlo mai — per te, pei tuoi puri occhi, muor Butterfly ... perchè tu possa andar di là dal mare senza che ti rimorda ai dì maturi, il materno abbandono. O a me, sceso dal trono dell'alto paradiso, guarda ben fiso, fiso di tua madre la faccia! che ten resti una traccia, guarda ben! Amore, addio! addio! piccolo amor! Va, gioca, gioca!

BUTTERFLY: You? You? You? You? You? You? You? My little god! Darling, my darling, lily and rose blossom. May you never learn that for your sake, for the sake of your innocent eyes, Butterfly must die ... so that you can go across the sea and never feel remorse, when you are grown up, for having deserted your mother. Oh, you that have come down to me from high heaven's throne, look hard, look hard at your mother's face, so that some

trace of it will stay with you.
Look hard! Darling, goodbye!
Goodbye! My little darling!
Go, play, play!

She seats him on a stool, gives him an American flag and a doll, and blindfolds him. Then she picks up the knife and goes behind the screen on which she had draped the white veil that covered the knife. The falling of the knife is heard and the veil is pulled down behind the screen. BUTTERFLY *emerges with the veil tied around her neck, gropes her way toward the baby and hugs him once more before she falls to the ground.*

PINKERTON *(from outside, approaching)*: Butterfly! Butterfly! Butterfly!

PINKERTON *(from outside, approaching)*: Butterfly! Butterfly! Butterfly!

PINKERTON *and* SHARPLESS *dash in.* BUTTERFLY *points to the baby and dies.* PINKERTON *kneels.* SHARPLESS, *sobbing, picks up the baby and kisses him.*

TRANSLATOR'S NOTES

TRANSLATOR'S NOTES

[1] On the names of the characters: *Chōchō* (or merely *chō*) is "butterfly" in Japanese; *san* is a suffix of respect. Kate is named Adelaide in Long's original story. Although the name Benjamin Franklin Pinkerton, created by Long, appears in full in the libretto (but see also note 12 below), the Italian scores (not followed here in this particular) constantly give his initials as F. B., presumably to avoid the British inference of "bloody fool." In German productions, it is the character's *last* name that is changed—to Linkerton, to avoid associations with the verb *pinkeln*, "to pee."

[2] The story and play specify Higashi Hill, an actual locality. A house there is now shown to tourists as being Butterfly's, but it is a substantial Victorian villa, built for a wealthy Englishman, and not the "accordion"-like house of the opera.

[3] Here, in a passage cut after the Brescia performance (all the alterations mentioned in these notes fall into this category), Pinkerton laughed at the servants' names and said he would just call them Ugly Mug 1, 2 and 3.

[4] Although the bonze *does* show up at the wedding, this grandmother never does. She appears to be a vestigial appendage from the story and play, in which Butterfly is completely orphaned and is supporting her *grandmother* by performing as a geisha.

[5] Long's story specifies that the 999-year lease was the only sort available to a foreigner. It could be canceled merely by nonpayment of the monthly rent.

[6] Untranslatable Italian pun. *Cotto*, "infatuated," literally means "cooked," so *grado di cottura*, "degree of infatuation," is also "cooking temperature."

[7] This is a familiar singular imperative, as if Butterfly were addressing only one friend (perhaps used just to rhyme with *vetta*).

[8] Geishas ("artistic persons") are women specially trained to entertain gentlemen with song and dance, generally in teahouses.

[9] Up to 1906, Butterfly continued with a description of her priestly uncle and her stupid, drunken uncle.

[10] Up to 1906, Pinkerton continued with an order to serve his Japanese guests the sort of repellent food he thought they would like, such as "spiders and candied flies."

[11] Because of the cut referred to in note 9 above, this uncle has never yet been mentioned, so that Pinkerton should not be able to recognize him.

[12] Up to 1906, Butterfly here introduced her mother, cousin and uncle (Yakusidé) to Pinkerton. The cousin also had a little son with her. Then Sharpless introduced the Commissioner (named Takasago) and the Registrar (named Hanako) to Pinkerton, whom he called Sir Francis Blummy Pinkerton! This version of the name, repeated later in the marriage-contract and letter scenes, where "Benjamin Franklin" was afterward substituted, satisfactorily explains the "F. B." still used in other passages in the Italian scores up to this day, but is otherwise totally unsatisfactory. After the introductions, Pinkerton asked Butterfly *not* whether she liked the house, but whether she *dis*liked the refreshments (her obvious discomfort being actually caused by her hesitation to reveal the objects hidden in her sleeves).

[13] The libretto never explains the Mikado's "invitation" to Butterfly's father. The Belasco play states, somewhat lamely, that he was a military man who had suffered an ignominious defeat. The original short story specifies that he had participated in the Satsuma Rebellion of 1877 (which helps to date the events narrated, Butterfly's age being given in the story as seventeen when Pinkerton returns). This rebellion, centered in the west of Japan, was the last significant challenge of the old feudal nobility to the progressive new Meiji regime that was sapping their privileges in the cause of centralization.

[14] This sentence was a later replacement for "You spent a hundred yen for me, but I'll be a thrifty housewife," which was still in the Brescia version.

[15] The word *forse* ("perhaps") was a replacement for *quasi* ("almost"), and *Amore mio!* (which spoils the rhyme scheme) replaced *E questi: via!* ("And as for these [the figurines], away with them!"). Although Butterfly says she has converted, nowhere in the course of the opera does she think or act like a Christian, nor does she have any further communication with missionaries, who most

likely would have aided her in her poverty. The play is silent about conversion, and in the story she merely considered it (her family's rejection of her being based on other grounds). Here the librettists sacrificed logic to pathos. Nor do they say to which sect of Christianity she converted. Interestingly, Nagasaki was the chief center of Roman Catholicism in Japan, while the other atom-bomb target, Hiroshima, was a Lutheran stronghold.

[16] Unnamed in the story, the ship was the *Connecticut* in the play.

[17] In the Brescia version the words *ed ella* were separated from *per consenso* by a brief uproar caused by the cousin and her child.

[18] Up to 1906, Pinkerton here toasted, and offered refreshments to, Butterfly's relatives individually, with comments from Yakusidé.

[19] *Kami* is actually the generic designation for the gods of Shinto, the indigenous Japanese religion. Folk religion in Japan mingles many different historic beliefs, and it might not be absolutely impossible for a Buddhist priest to call on the *kami* (apparently considered as the name of an individual god in the opera), but he would more likely allude to the numerous Buddhist divinities. In fact, the librettists' Japanese pantheon is not to be taken seriously at all. Later on, in Suzuki's prayers, *Izaghi ed Izanami* probably reflects the actual Izanagi and Izanami, a pair of progenitor deities from a very early stratum of Japanese religon.

[20] An *obi*, of course, is the sash worn with a *kimono*, not the robe itself. Oddly, the librettists have made *obi* a feminine (Italian) noun here and a masculine noun when it recurs in the next act.

[21] Up to 1906, Butterfly here related that she was already thinking of getting married, even temporarily, when Goro suggested Pinkerton, and that the idea of Pinkerton as a husband frightened her at first because he was a strange "barbarian." The cutting of this passage, which illuminated some of Butterfly's background, left an awkward gap both textually and musically in the final version of the opera.

[22] The "robins nesting again" idea is also important in the story and the play. It would seem that Pinkerton, who in the story is repeatedly shown to be addicted to recent popular music (he sings parody versions of "Rock-a-Bye Baby," published 1887, and "She Is the Belle of New York" from the 1897 musical comedy *The Belle of New York*), was humorously referring to a song here as well: the

very popular 1883 song "When the Robins Nest Again," words and music by Frank Howard.

[23] Often appears as *sull'estremo* ("at the farthest").

[24] In the Belasco play, Yamadori (as in the story, a resident of New York City) wore elegant Western dress and spoke English with the utmost refinement.

[25] The orchestral score has *guadagnarsi* ("earn *her* [bread and clothing]"), a less interesting reading. Up to 1906, the remainder of the aria after the words *impietosite genti* was totally different. Instead of bewailing the street singer or geisha's lot and preferring death, Butterfly imagined that she would publicly dance and sing a song about the Japanese gods, that the Emperor would pass by, that she would show him her beautiful baby and that he would perhaps make the baby "the handsomest prince in his kingdom."

[26] The short story and play state that it is normal for Japanese babies to be given a temporary name until a suitable occasion arises to give them a permanent one.

[27] Cuts were made here even before the Opéra-Comique production. In Milan and Brescia, before Butterfly said *Due ore forse*, she said *Certo di più* ("Of course it will be more"). Then, after *faville*, she had a short passage, based on the story, about wanting to light lanterns but being unable to afford them.

[28] In a brief passage cut here (based on lines in the story), Suzuki recommended rest as a restorative of beauty.

[29] This passage of Butterfly's was originally longer, but no substantial matter was cut.

[30] At this point, Butterfly originally sang an uninteresting little children's song to Trouble.

[31] In 1904, Suzuki said *Già l'alba!* ("Dawn already!") and Butterfly said *Verrà ... verrà col pieno sole* ("He'll come ... he'll come when the sun has completely risen"). Puccini changed this so that the scene could start right off with stronger lighting.

[32] In the short story, Mrs. Pinkerton arrived in Nagasaki by passenger steamer a week after her husband—she did not have to travel on the gunboat!

[33] *Piangete* is a polite or plural form of the verb, implying that Suzuki (always addressed in the familiar singular) is not supposed to be the only one weeping.

[34] One of the most important changes made for the Opéra-

Comique version (the occasion of most of the alterations made in the interests of good taste and propriety) begins with this speech of Butterfly's. The purpose of the change was to transfer to Sharpless the request for the baby originally made by Kate, and to soften Butterfly's reactions to Kate. The original passage deserves full translation:

> BUTTERFLY: Ah! That blonde woman makes me so scared! So scared!
>
> KATE: I am the innocent cause of all your misfortunes. Forgive me.
>
> BUTTERFLY: Don't touch me! How long is it since he married *you?*
>
> KATE: A year. And won't you let me do anything for the child? I'll treat him with loving care. It's a sad thing, a sad thing, but do it for his good.
>
> BUTTERFLY: Who knows? Everything is finished now!

The definitive text matches up with the original again at Kate's speech *Potete perdonarmi, Butterfly?* ("Can you ever forgive me, Butterfly?").

³⁵ A cut here, made at the same time:

> BUTTERFLY: But I'd like you to tell him ... that I shall find peace ...
>
> KATE: Your hand, ... would you give me your hand?
>
> BUTTERFLY: Please, that—no. Go now.

³⁶ Another cut made then: Sharpless offers Butterfly the money Pinkerton had given him for her (an action originally performed at the words *Datele voi qualche soccorso*, slightly before the number "Addio, fiorito asil"), but Butterfly refuses, saying also that her new certainty about her situation will give her greater peace than her hopes and dreams did. When Sharpless asks if he may see her again, she invites him, too, to return in half an hour. This is the explanation for his arrival with Pinkerton at the end; in the definitive text, only Pinkerton and Kate have been invited back.

³⁷ In a passage cut at this point, Butterfly reminded Suzuki that the latter had recommended a beauty rest (in a passage also cut; see note 28 above), and said that she was now going to get that rest. She also quoted an old song about death.